Good for a Laugh

Six funny stories and their playscript versions with lyrics and basic music in tonic sol-fa. For amateur production with camcorder, DVD, CD or film. These are all suitable for stage, schools, village halls, colleges, hotels, gardens or in your own home. The stories include humorous tales of many different types - skits, farces, sketches, slapstick, witty humor and satire. Scripts and stories include:

☺ A single man feels left out in
Do You Serve Singles?

☺ Relatives can't help quarrelling in
The Viewing of Auntie Agatha.

☺ False detectives go on the make in
Detectives Only Joking?

☺ A young man suffers embarrassment in
Sore Bottom.

☺ Three prospectors are visited by a conman and Professor Luck in
Hope and Go Seek.

☺ Thieves form a trade union in
The International Convention of Burglars.

LIFE OF DREW CARSON

Storyteller and Songwriter

Sam Drew Carson was born in the North of Ireland and educated there at Wellington College and the Ulster Polytechnic. He completed his education in the USA at New Mexico Highlands University and the University of Arkansas. He has traveled widely in Europe, around the Atlantic and in North America.

Carson worked as a seaman and fish-gutter in Vestmannaeyjar off the coast of Iceland.

He has lived and worked in the Irish and Western Isles Gaeltachts and was married in Welsh-speaking Carmarthen after which he honeymooned in Belfast.

He has told his stories, composed and sung his songs, seeking storylines in Bristol and the English Westcountry.

Carson has also lived and written in Nashville, Tennessee, in the wooded hills of Mid-America and from the Appalachians to the Ozarks. This was the culture that gave rise to the now worldwide Scotch-Irish country music.

In the USA, he has also worked beside the bayous of the French-speaking Cajuns in the South and among the Western Spanish-speaking Navajos, Apaches and Pueblos of the Sangre de Cristo Mountains in New Mexico.

Carson has sailed far into the seas of old Gaelic and Oriental legend. After many years searching for inspiration for story and music, the author is still traveling and writing.

BOOKS BY THE SAME AUTHOR

ZENISUB - *Fun and Games in Businezz*

SAGA OF TSUNAMI - *the Trilogy, 2nd edition*

GOOD FOR A LAUGH - *Six Funny Playscripts for Amateurs*

DARK SHADOWS - *Six Amateur Playscripts of Mystery and the Night*

SNOWING CATS AND DOGS - *Four Playscripts of the New Year Season for Amateurs*

FOR OLDTIMES SAKE - *Four Nostalgic Playscripts for Amateurs*

MYSTERY OF THE MISSING TRAVELERS

MYSTERY OF THE WEREWOLF MURDERS

TWO LADIES OF MYSTERY

THREE TIME-TRAVEL MYSTERIES

EUROPEAN LYRICS - *French, Spanish and Gaelic Classics*

COMMON WEALTH - *the Growth and Fair Spread of Money*

Good for a Laugh

Six Funny Playscripts for Amateurs

DREW CARSON

Order from:
https://www.createspace.com/3491390

Legals

Published by S. A. Carson,
29 Northleaze, Long Ashton, Bristol BS41 9HS, UK
Publisher's email: verygoodreading@googlemail.com

STORIES/PLAYSCRIPTS: *Detectives Only Joking? The Viewing of Auntie Agatha, The International Convention of Burglars, Do You Serve Singles? Sore Bottom, Hope and Go Seek (same plot as Old Professor Luck, q.v.).*

ISBN: 978-0-9561435-3-2

TABLE OF CONTENTS

DO YOU SERVE SINGLES?

A Short Story and a One-Act Play

The Story

The sign outside read 'Family Restaurant'. It was a small cozy eatery in the dining room of which were several tables covered in tablecloths and set for meals. Each table, depending on size, had two to six chairs surrounding it. There was carpet or colored linoleum on the floor. The walls were decorated with artifacts of family life, like pictures of children and babies and children's fictional characters such as pirates, Santa Claus, fairies, nursery rhyme characters. The restaurant was in the middle range of eatery, not fast food or quick or casual, but not gourmet either.

This was a middle-class family restaurant with waiter and waitress service. At the back of the dining room were double doors leading to the kitchen. There were signs saying – 'Exit' on the right and 'Entrance' on the left.

On the left hand side at one of the tables sat a family of five consisting of a large fat mother and three large children. Squashed between the fat mother and the children was a tiny and inconspicuous father - small and skinny. He could have been mistaken for a child. This family were quietly eating and conversing in a low key, nodding to each other.

In the middle of the dining room sat a well dressed respectable looking middle-aged lady, engrossed in eating and reading a paper.

The waiter hovered around officiously, dusting off tables and chairs, standing erect, smiling at the patrons, humming lightly and generally making himself available and affable.

Just then, an elderly woman came in. She was a tall, thin aristocrat, dressed in tweeds, broad-brimmed hat, heavy stockings and wearing large flat shoes. She was an old-fashioned country lady with a leather briefcase and walking cane. She sat at one of the laid-out tables. The waiter, pencil and notepad in hand, scurried over, obsequiously bowing and scraping and writing down every word of her order.

"Your ladyship, your highness, how can we serve you? It's such a great privilege . . yes, yes, Ma'am."

At about the same time, a single man came in. He was a youngish 25-45 raffish, elegant man, well and respectably dressed in good clothes. He had short cut hair, a moustache but was otherwise clean shaven. The young man looked around disdainfully, shrugged at what he saw, which evidently did not greatly impress him. However, he finally selected a chair and table. He sat down, rubbed his hands together and looked expectantly at the waiter who ignored him to deal with the older lady. The single man looked outraged, taken aback, scared, insulted, shocked, each time the waiter spoke to the old lady, who noted these reactions and responded with suspicion directed towards the waiter. The waiter was unaware of the single man's bad influence. The single man made funny faces and wiggled his fingers with thumbs in ears.

The old lady spoke with a crisp upper-class accent, "I'd like a nice cup of tea - not any old tea, mind you . . ."

The waiter replied obsequiously, "No Ma'am, nice tea, a proper cuppa."

The old lady reprimanded him, "Don't mutter, I'm deaf – the tea must be of the caliber of Earl Grey."

The waiter asked, "Who?"

The old lady stared fixedly at the tablecloth, "Earl Grey," she intoned, "Earl Grey."

Not understanding, the waiter lifted up the tablecloth and peeked underneath. He shrugged in mystification and mumbled, "No one there."

"Of course, he's not under the table you fool. My neck is a little stiff today. I mean I want some tea of Earl Grey caliber."

The waiter, writing assiduously, bowed and scraped, "Yes, your grace, your ladyship, 'Earl Grey caliber.' I understand."

The old lady was pleased, "Yes, or orange Pekoe High Grade - not too weak nor too strong - not too dark nor too light. Just a nice medium orange-brown Pekoe, with a tea-ish smell."

The waiter continued writing, "Certainly your ladyship - medium orange-brown Peekaboo, tea-ish flavor."

The old lady smiled, "Yes, that's correct. Also a plate of fresh french fries - also medium-cooked to a nice light brown or pale honey color."

The waiter continued to nod and write conscientiously, "Yes, My Lady - light brown french fries, medium done."

"Oh, I'm so glad you are trying to get it right," she beamed, "You're so attentive. Such a nice chap - but still, read it all back to me loudly to make sure it's all correct."

The old lady blinked and beamed, then put her hand to her ear, listening with approval and pleasure as the waiter smiled and nodded and read back loudly.

"Yes, your Ladyship," the waiter fawned, "And it's so kind of you to give us your patronage, Ma'am. Yes . . not strong not weak, nice middling strong orangie Peekaboo or Earl Grey Tea with a plate of honey browned medium done french fries. Is that correct My Lady?"

At this she nodded with great satisfaction. "Oh, I do so like the truly family atmosphere here. I feel so much at home. Home is in the very air."

The waiter bowed, backed away, turned, walked briskly to the kitchen doors, opened them a little then cried loudly and vulgarly to someone in the kitchen, "Chips and tea for the old bag."

The old lady jumped up and gathered her belongings, "How dare you, you oaf, you ape, you village imbecile."

She shook her cane at the waiter, threateningly. The waiter's jaw dropped and he stumbled in surprise, as he hissed, "You old phony. I thought you said you were deaf? . . . I mean . . at your age you should be deaf . . . I'm awfully sorry . . I mean." Suddenly he thought of a bright idea. "That's the way we treat all our customers. See, this is a family cafe. Families insult each other all the time, you must agree. It's just familyism M'Lady.

"See, its called streamline ordering . . . Ah . . it's in the latest book on *Fasttrack to Success*, Ma'am."

"Oh, really. Familyism eh? Streamline insults, eh? I will now do an act of streamline walkout."

The waiter dashed back to the service door and returned with tea and chips. He placed these on the table.

"Ma'am, the payment? Our tea and french fries are now ready? See?"

The old lady squinted at the tea, "That tea has a dead fly in it."

The waiter smugly responded, "Yes, Ma'am, we pride ourselves on our free organic supplement, M'Lady."

At this, the offended customer indignantly walked out. "Oh I see, well, give the tea and chips, with all their crawling organic components, to the author of the latest success book - and let him pay for them." She squirmed at the thought, flicked her hand and left.

The waiter then saw the single man for the first time and rushed over to his side. He began to bow and scrape with nods and smiles. He handed a menu to the young man who languidly looked over it with raised eyebrows, nodding and shaking his head at this or that item while scratching his chin, pushing back his eyebrows, pressing down the hair on the back of his neck. The single man was bored.

Eventually he raised his head with eyes closed and passed his left hand across his forehead and left temple as though deeply in thought. He opened his eyes and saw the waiter as for the first time.

"Ah, waiter - here you are - dear chap. Ha, Ha, I knew you were there somewhere. Ah yes, waiter." He paused, speaking to himself. "Yes, hmm. Just say no to more bread."

The waiter produced his notebook and pencil and waited expectantly, "Yes Sir?"

The single man then opened his eyes wide, stared at the menu and hit his forehead with the heel of his left hand. "Oh my goodness. Waiter you're not going to serve me are you? Oh, I'm sorry, I'm so sorry my dear fellow, coming in here, just because I had plenty of money and I was hungry and wanted a meal, how foolish of me. I do apologize, waiter, old boy. I see this is a family restaurant." He looked around and considered the pictures and artifacts. He rose as one about to leave.

"But what's wrong with us, Sir? We serve very good food, our prices are very competitive." He lowered his voice and muttered, "Compared to the Taj Mahal or the White House."

The single man shook his head sadly, still standing, "Oh, but you see I'm not eligible - I'm single. Sorry old chum and all that . . ."

The waiter was relieved to hear this, "Oh, I see. But that's all right. Why that's just fine, Sir. That doesn't matter at all."

The single man sat down puzzled, "Really? It doesn't matter?"

The waiter wiped the table smugly, "No, No."

Nevertheless, the single man was puzzled, "But perhaps you don't grasp my full point, dear chap. I'm not a family man, my parents are dead. I've no brothers or sisters – I'm single - unmarried. Surely you can't be thinking of serving me in a family restaurant? Why, I even live on my own, old boy."

The waiter, spread his hands in a gesture of tolerance, "That's all right, Sir, we'll still serve you."

The single man stared severely at the waiter, "Is the owner or manager aware of this tolerant policy, dear boy?"

"Oh yes Sir, it's just fine with us. I'm part owner."

"Then why is this place called a family restaurant. Isn't that very misleading?"

"Well Sir, I suppose the word family conjures up pleasant thoughts. It's a nice name - family folks are good souls you know, Sir."

The single man disagreed, "I don't know about that. Ghengis Khan, Winston Churchill, Cesar Borgia and Josef Stalin were all family men, whereas lots of single men like me are perfectly decent souls. Wouldn't you agree, dear chap?"

"Certainly Sir. A family restaurant simply means . . ." He thought, hesitated and then with sudden light dawning on him, "We serve families." The waiter was pleased and beamed at his shrewd understanding of the usage.

The young man raised his eyebrows and smiled as one suddenly enlightened, "Ah now I see, I see - you serve families."

The waiter laughed, pleased to have made his point, "Yes Sir, we serve families. Yes."

The single man rubbed his hands together, "Ah, now I see, old chap. Well, good, in that case just serve me up a wife and two kids will you, there's a good fellow. I'm tired of being single anyhow. It can be lonely you know - yes, just serve me with a wife and one or two kids - one will do fine."

The waiter was confused, "But Sir, I do not mean that we provide families." He reconsidered and brightened, "But, if you bring your own then we'll serve them with a meal. See?"

The single man reacted very sternly, "Look here. This is a family restaurant, right waiter."

"Yes Sir."

The single man was adamant, "Then I want a family. Now are you going to get me a family or are you not?"

The waiter looked around, embarrassed, "Shush, quiet, Sir. We can't do that. You need to bring your own family and then we'll serve them."

The single man slapped his knee and held up his right index finger, "Right, that's what I said all along - that's what I said to begin with. Right? You don't want single men here. I have to provide my own family. Isn't that true?"

By now the waiter was confused and scratched his head, "Well, I suppose so, Sir."

"See. This is discrimination against the single man. Why should I have to get my own family when all the worst rogues in the world have got families?"

"Sir! I'm lost," uttered the waiter.

The single man continued adamantly, "Very well. So you admit I'm right? You do discriminate against singles, eh? Just as I said to begin with, right?" He stood up, " I'm afraid I'll have to leave in protest."

The waiter bowed and threw his hands wide in confusion, shaking his head.

The single man was about to leave, having turned away from his table. The waiter jumped between the single man and the door and pleaded with him to reconsider.

"Now, Sir, please feel free to leave if you don't like the place or the fare - that is your privilege, but, Sir, I wouldn't want you to leave on a misunderstanding. Please sit down and let me explain. You see, Sir, I'm part-owner of this restaurant and I need the business - you see I've a family to support - I have a wife and three kids too."

The young man suddenly became interested and alert and sat down again. "Oh, so you're a family man, old chap. Now I'm beginning to see the picture. That explains a lot."

The waiter was pleased, "Yes, Sir. I have children to feed."

But the customer reacted ironically, "So let them eat here free of charge - what, old boy?"

The waiter was horrified, "What - at these prices? Oh, I couldn't afford that Sir."

"Ah, so I should pay these prices but not you - because you're a family man, dear chap, eh? And I'm just a victimized, hated, spat upon, loathed single person, eh? I'm to be ripped off and exploited and gouged out from the inmost guts but not you or your nice little family. See what I mean?"

"Dear, dear, do let me explain," replied the waiter, "It's not discrimination. My family is too poor to eat here and we just call it a family cafe because it seemed like a good healthy image – it's just a wholesome business persona. See Sir?"

The young man coolly looked at his nails, "Yes my dear chap I do see."

The waiter smiled, fawned and nodded.

"Yes I do see – it's a healthy image - but me, I'm single, so I'm unhealthy, is that it? I'm a freak eh? So there's something abnormal about me - is that the way of it dear fellow - because I'm single, I'm an oddity. Yes? Go ahead, be honest, say it, there's something wrong with me – that's it, isn't it. Say it. Say it and I'll knock your oafish head off. Go ahead, say so, say I'm a weirdo . . . I dare you."

The waiter was horrified at this unexpected response, "No, No, Sir. I never thought it for a moment. It's just that 'family' seems to mean 'good' to a lot of people. Single is good too, Sir, of course, naturally - why my brother Tom is single and he hasn't been in jail for years – he's a fine reformed person."

The young man sneered, "Ahh! A Jailbird - I knew it, you associate singles with criminals. That's it, now I see it. We're the rejects of society - the castaways of life, marooned on desert islands of social isolation where we will trouble no one's conscience."

The young man thumped the table in despair. He pointed a finger of accusation at the waiter. Other diners glanced up briefly and then returned to their meals, quiet talk and books.

The man continued his diatribe, getting more and more hysterical with every word, "You, you force me to pay more tax than you do while you squirm out of your fiscal duty just because you have kids, eh? Why should I pay more tax just because you have been improvident and reckless and couldn't care less? Why should I support you and yours, why should you get all the breaks and handouts while all I get is abuse and accusations of being a freaked out whacko eh?

"Oh no, dear boy, so families are good eh, what about the crime families. What about all you married men who started wars and sent out us poor single blokes to fight for you.

"Oh yes, single is bad, family is good, is it? You family men get all the days off for sick kids. You rob and get caught - you did it to feed your kids. Oh yes. You skipped class in college, didn't do your homework, you avoided the auditor, the health inspector - all because your Ma supposedly died or your granny or your brat was sick. Isn't that the truth?

"How many Ma's or Granmas or brats have you had die to cover up and help you hide from your blunders? You hide behind your family, don't you and so, naturally, family is a good image you say - I think it's a terrible word."

The waiter looked around in fear. He was at his wits end to placate the disgruntled customer. "Well, there's good families and bad families but look, what you say has made me think - maybe you're right – 'family' can be taken either way, so maybe we'll change the name of the cafe to say, healthy or health food or goodies - how about that – we'll leave out the word 'family.' How about that Sir?"

The customer was horrified and pointed at the waiter, "Oh so you'll change the name, dear boy, will you? Leave out the word 'family,' eh?"

The waiter nodded happily as the customer continued.

"So that's it - change the mere name and catch out people like me unawares, eh? Entrap us, mislead us, get us in here on false pretences and then insult us and rip us off - oh, no, oh no Sir - never - never - never will I bow to that kind of deceit and decrepit deception – I'll expose you as a true family eatery at heart. I'll never let you get away with it. I'll write to the world press. I'll show you up for what you really are - a family man." He slowly and sinisterly pointed a finger at the waiter.

"So, so, I'll not change the name - if it makes you happy. I'll keep the name 'family.' All right, all right. Family restaurant."

The young man sneered in triumph, "I knew it. Familyism survives after all. I can see the headlines. Familyism wins again. Oh, it's too terrible. Oh it's too much. Familyism rules the waves."

The young man sobbed as the waiter gasped and raised his head and hands in despair. The other customers looked slightly embarrassed and exchanged odd glances.

Desperately, the waiter tried to calm down the situation by murmuring, "Cheer up, Sir. This is just a good old fashioned caff." He patted the young man on the shoulder.

"There, there, Sir - Cheer up. Tell you what, you can have anything, anything in the house, Sir, at half price." The waiter pointed to the various items on the menu.

The single man continued moaning, "Oh, it's so tough being single - no grandchildren to play with, no measles to get the victory over, no summer camps to watch the dear little kids at. No school events to thrill one - see what I mean dear fellow? No grandpa to fall down my stairs. No brother to kick me . . ."

The waiter became sympathetic, "I know Sir. No little girls with little curls, no little boys with little toys - but that's why I'm offering you anything in the house at half-price, that's to compensate you for being caught out in a family cafe." The waiter mumbled to himself, "the prices are already double what they should be anyway."

The single man began to cheer up, "Half-price, old boy. That's jolly decent of you and all that, old chap!"

The young man began to study the menu but his eyes slowly drifted above it to the family seated at the corner table where the large wife and kids still tended to obscure the small father. The young man's eyes focused on this family group. While the waiter, suspecting something strange, based on his immediate experience of the young man, covered his eyes and groaned.

"Oh, no, no, please no."

But the single man persisted, "Yes, I need a wife and family. How much is that wife and family over there?" He pointed to the corner family group while the waiter began dusting the table furiously in nervous agitation. "How much?"

"But Sir, they're not for sale. I can't just sell them to you, Sir. They're not mine!"

The single man raised his voice and pointed to the family group, "No – they're mine from now on. Hey you, wife and children, I'll have you, if you don't mind, at half price too."

The wife stood up and shielded her husband, "What on earth do you mean?"

The young man explained wearily, "I'm tired of being single. I just want to buy you all as my wife and children since the waiter here has put you on offer, O.K?"

The small husband came out from behind his wife and marched towards the door, past the waiter and the single man, beckoning his wife and children after him. They all marched out as the other lady diner looked concerned and surprised.

The small husband declared, "How dare you, young feller, these are my wife and kids and not for sale, Sir."

The family group began to march out with their heads in the air followed by the small husband.

The young man cried out to the husband, "I beg your pardon. I didn't see you, Sir!"

The husband replied, "So I'm a dwarf, am I? Yes?"

At this point the waiter called after the departing group, "But you haven't paid Sir."

The large wife, while walking out, threw out one last departing shot, "After that insult you should pay us!"

As the family all left, the waiter dropped his towel in despair and weakly staggered against a table, one hand on his head, his mouth open, his other hand on the table to steady himself and prevent him from fainting.

The single man now turned his attention to the middle-aged, well dressed diner who still remained at a table in the middle of the dining room. "Can I have that one instead? At half-price?"

The waiter gasped, "But she's a respectable lady, Sir."

The middle-aged lady was horrified at these remarks and began to gather together her belongings and put on her hat and coat.

These remarks continued loudly, between the waiter and the single man.

"Of course, she's a respectable lady. It was you who put her on sale at half-price, not me. I can see she's a respectable lady - what other kind of wife do you think I would want, old fellow, eh? Do I look like a chap who would want to marry a brazen hussy, a painted floozy, a trollopy tart, a shameless, sleazy slum-slut - for a wife? So that is what you think of me, eh? So . . you stand there accusing me of being a low-class, slam, ram, bam slimy slob with no discretion or civilized discrimination. Do you; oh, really?"

He began to clasp and unclasp his hands hysterically, pushing back his sleeve aggressively and standing as one looking for a fight. "Am I like that, waiter, Old Boy, am I?"

The waiter backed away, fearfully, "Oh dear no, no, no, Sir. It's just the time, the place, the occasion - is not appropriate. You know Sir – it's nothing personal against you, Sir, but the lady is really quite young, barely middle-aged, genteel and attractive."

The single man responded indignantly, "Ah, now I understand. You think that I'm an impoverished, penniless, desperate and despicable starveling who would grasp at the bones of any lean cadaver of marital rejection. So I'm the one who would seize any scraggy bag of withered bones, a dried-up immolated hag, a skinny shriveled-up old crone moaning and groaning and creaking and squeaking like a wooden floor or door - a scrawny mummy - you think I deserve a wife like that - that - THAT'S what you're saying, isn't it? Admit it? You think this lady is too good for me, eh?"

"I never even thought of such a vile thing, Sir. My mind is set on a very simple, business matter, I assure you, my dear Sir."

"And just what is that simple business matter, my good fellow?"

Naively the waiter answered, "Why, food for money, Sir. Just that, a restaurant, an eatery, food for money. Simple - see?"

The waiter spread his hand helplessly as the young man calmed down and replied, "Oh, I see, quite well, old boy. Well, you made the offer you know. Remember? Anything in the house - half-price and all that. So, can I have her then?"

The lady began to walk past the two disputants in disgust.

"Oh, lady, come back, on second thoughts I'll pay full price for you as a wife."

The waiter remonstrated with the single man, "Oh, but I meant food and drink only."

"But Ma'am, your check!" he shouted after the lady who was walking out.

"Check? That's a joke - check him out," she motioned to the single man. "He's the freako who needs it!"

The waiter called after her, "Yes, Ma'am, I agree."

The single man cried out, "Oh do you indeed - so I'm a kinko? Am I? I knew that was what you were trying to say all along. How dare you! Family Restaurant indeed. I'll never set foot in another brat-based cafe in my life."

The single man stomped out in disgust as the waiter called after him, "Oh, thank you Sir. I'll hold you to that promise."

The waiter looked around in distress at the empty dining room, sighed, sobbed, wiped his eyes with his left hand and waved his right hand outwards in a gesture of despair. "Now, how am I going to feed my wife and children? Oh my poor family."

END OF STORY

The Playscript

PRODUCTION SPECIFICATIONS

Nine Actors:

Three male, three female and three children.

One Set:

The same for all three scenes.

Age Groups:

All.

Music:

Three songs: *Drink Your Tea, Food Ain't As Good As Before, Fish and Chips.*

Stage Time:

Approximately 30-40 minutes.

OUTLINE OF THE PLAY

Scene One:

Singles are Bad, eh?

Scene Two:

Families are Good, eh?

Scene Three:

But Wives and Kids are Real.

CHARACTERS IN THE PLAY

SINGLE MAN:

A customer in a family cafe.

WAITER:

Formally dressed in evening wear.

HUSBAND:

A short, thin man.

WIFE:

Tall, mature and heavily built.

ELDERLY WOMAN:

Tall and aristocratic country lady

MID-AGED LADY:

Well dressed and highly respectable - business type.

THREE CHILDREN:

Of any size or gender.

****

SCENE ONE - SINGLES ARE BAD, EH?

Scene: *The dining room of a restaurant. Several tables are covered in tablecloths and set for meals. Each table, depending on size, has two to six chairs surrounding it. There is carpet or colored linoleum on the floor and the walls are decorated with pictures or artifacts according to the theme of the restaurant, which is something in the middle range of eatery - not fast food or quick or casual but not gourmet either.*

The themes should be related to families, e.g., pictures of children and babies and children's fictional characters such as pirates, Santa Claus, fairies, nursery rhyme characters. This is a middle class family restaurant with waiter or waitress service. Along the backdrop are double doors leading to the kitchen. Signs saying – 'Exit' on the right and 'Entrance' on the left.

In practice, the usual right and left-stage entrances will be used by all characters in some productions. At the far left down-stage at one of the tables is a family of five consisting of a large fat mother and three large children of any age. Squashed between the fat mother and the children is a tiny and inconspicuous father - small and skinny. He should be mistaken for a child until his exit line later in the play. This family are quietly eating and conversing quietly and nodding to each other.

Just left of center is a well dressed respectable looking middle-aged lady, engrossed in eating and reading a paper or book. The clothes of all characters should be contemporary.

***Enter left, the Waiter (male or female)** and hovers around mid-stage officiously, dusting off tables or chairs, standing erect, smiling at the patrons, humming lightly and generally making himself available and affable for about a minute or two until . . .*

***Enter left, an Elderly Woman,** tall, thin and aristocratic, in tweeds and large hat, heavy stockings and large flat shoes; an old-fashioned country lady with a leather briefcase and walking cane. She sits at any one of the laid tables. Waiter,* *pencil and notepad in hand, scurries over, obsequiously bowing and scraping and writing down every word of her order.*

WAITER: Your ladyship, your highness, how can we serve you? It's such a great privilege . . yes, yes, Ma'am.

***Enter right, Single Man**, a youngish 25-45 raffish, elegant man, well and respectably dressed in good clothes, with short cut hair, perhaps a moustache but otherwise clean shaven. The young man looks around disdainfully, shrugs at what he sees, which evidently does not greatly impress him and finally selects a chair and table, right of center. He sits, rubs his hands together and looks expectantly at the waiter who ignores him to deal with Old Lady. Single man looks outraged, taken aback, scared, insulted, shocked each time the waiter speaks to Old Lady. Old Lady notes these reactions and responds with suspicion directed towards waiter who is unaware of Single Man's bad influence. Single Man makes funny faces, wiggles his fingers with thumb in ears or on nose and so on.*

OLD LADY: *(in a crisp upper-class accent)* I'd like a nice cup of tea - not any old tea, mind you . . .

WAITER: No Ma'am, nice tea, a proper cuppa.

OLD LADY: Don't mutter, I'm deaf - it must be of the caliber of Earl Grey.

WAITER: Who?

OLD LADY: *(staring at the tablecloth)* Earl Grey, Earl Grey.

Waiter lifts up the tablecloth and peeks underneath. He looks at the audience and shrugs in mystification.

WAITER: *(to audience)* No one there.

OLD LADY: He's not under the table you fool. My neck is a little stiff today. I mean I want some tea of Earl Grey caliber.

WAITER: *(writing and bowing and scraping)* Yes, your grace, your ladyship, "Earl Grey caliber." I understand.

OLD LADY: Or orange Pekoe High Grade - not too weak nor too strong - not too dark nor too light. Just a nice medium orange-brown Pekoe, with a tea-ish smell.

WAITER: *(writing assiduously)* Certainly your ladyship - medium orange-brown Pekoe, tea-ish flavor.

OLD LADY: *(pleased)* Yes, that's correct. Also a plate of fresh french fries - also medium-cooked to a nice light brown or pale honey color.

WAITER: *(still nodding and writing)* Yes, my lady - light brown french fries, medium done.

OLD LADY: *(beaming)* Oh, I'm so glad you are trying to get it right. You're so attentive. Such a nice chap. But still read it all back to me loudly to make sure it's all correct.

Old Lady blinks and beams, then puts her hand to her ear, listening with approval and pleasure as waiter smiles and nods and reads back loudly.

WAITER: Yes, your ladyship - and it's so kind of you to give us your patronage, Ma'am. Yes, *(reads)* . . not strong not weak, nice middling strong orangie Pekoe or Earl Grey Tea with a plate of honey browned medium done french fries. Is that correct my lady?

Sings **DRINK YOUR TEA**

Sung: Jolly

VERSE 1:

d d d d l_1 - d
Don't get scared or skittish
f f f r - f
Fight to the finish
d d d d r - d
Be proud to be British
d l_1 s_1
Drink your tea.
d d d d l_1 - d
No matter how you suffer
f f f f r - f
Keep a true stiff upper
f f f f m - m
Eat a good fish supper
f s f
Drink your tea.

VERSE 1
Don't get scared or skittish
Fight to the finish
Be proud to be British
Drink your tea
No matter how you suffer
Keep a true stiff upper
Eat a good fish supper
Drink your tea.

OLD LADY: *(she nods with great satisfaction)* Oh, I do so like the truly family atmosphere here. I feel so much at home. Home is in the very air.

Waiter bows, backs away, bows, turns, walks downstage briskly to kitchen doors, opens them a little.

WAITER: *(shouts loudly and bruskly to someone in the kitchen)* Chips and tea for the old bag.

OLD LADY: *(jumping and gathering her belongings)* How dare you, you oaf, you ape, you village imbecile.

The Old Lady shakes her cane at the waiter, threateningly. Waiter's jaw drops and he stumbles in surprise.

WAITER: You old phony. I thought you said you were deaf? . . I mean . . at your age you should be deaf . . . I'm awfully sorry . . I mean - *(thinking of a bright idea)* that's the way we treat all our customers. See, this is a family cafe. Families insult each other all the time, you must agree. *(the Old Lady glowers as the Waiter thinks of another bright idea)* It's just familyism M'Lady.
See, it's called streamline ordering . . . Ah . . it's in the latest book on *Fasttrack to Success,* Ma'am.

OLD LADY: Oh, really. Familyism eh? streamline insults, eh? I will now do an act of streamline walkout.

Waiter dashes back to service door and returns with tea and chips.

WAITER: Ma'am, the payment? Our tea and french fries are now ready? See?

OLD LADY: *(squinting at the tea)* That tea has a dead fly in it.

WAITER: *(smugly)* Yes, Ma'am we pride ourselves on our free organic supplement, M'Lady.

OLD LADY: *(indignantly walking off stage left)* Oh I see, well, give the tea and chips with all their crawling organic components *(she squirms)* to the author of the latest success book - and let him pay for them.

Old Lady flicks her hand and leaves left-stage.

The waiter now sees Single Man for the first time and rushes over to Single Man's side, just to the left of this previously unnoticed customer. The waiter begins to bow and scrape and nods and smiles and hands the young man a menu. The young man languidly looks over the menu with raised eyebrows, nodding or shaking his head at this or that item while scratching his chin or pushing back his eyebrows or pressing down the hair on the back of his neck. Single Man is bored.

Eventually, Single Man raises his head with eyes closed and passes his left hand across his forehead and left temple as though deeply in thought. He opens his eyes and sees the waiter as for the first time.

SINGLE MAN: Ah, waiter - Here you are - dear chap. Ha, Ha, I knew you were there somewhere. Ah yes, waiter . . . *(he pauses, speaking to himself)* Yes, hmm. Just say no to more bread.

The waiter produces his notebook and pencil and waits expectantly.

WAITER: Yes Sir?

Sings: **FOOD AIN'T AS GOOD AS BEFORE**

Sung: Slow

VERSE 1:

t_1 - r m m m - m r m s s s - l
I ain't shed no tears over onions in years

s - l t l s m r t_1 r
It seems that good smells have been banned

t_1 - r m m m - m r m s s s l
My taste bud's a dud when I eat a new spud

s - l t l s - m m m - m
And the eggs are so weak they can't stand

t r^1 t t - t l - s l l - l l
The dog that I had went a stark staring mad

s - l t l s - m r t_1 r
When it smelt a fresh steak from the store

t_1 - r m m m - m r - m s s s - l
Now the meat has no smell and the dog sleeps so well

s - l t l s - m m m - m
Oh the food ain't as good as before

Do You Serve Singles?

VERSE 1:
I ain't shed no tears over onions in years
It seems that good smells have been banned
My taste bud's a dud when I eat a new spud
And the eggs are so weak they can't stand
The dog that I had went a stark staring mad
When it smelt a fresh steak from the store
Now the meat has no smell and the dog sleeps so well
Oh the food ain't as good as before
No the food ain't as good as before.

VERSE 2:
The tomatoey smell was so strong I could tell
It had grown up on all loving care
And the scarred ugly fruit was so sweet and so cute
I was eager as a bee for my share
So let's get the good oldtime taste back in food
Must we wait for a pie in the sky?
Tell me, O tell, where is sharp taste and smell?
Where's the catfish that made the cat cry? *(sniff, sniff)*

REFRAIN: *(Tune: repeat last 4 lines of verse)*
I'm a-looking for good and plain old fashioned food
With a crunch or a munch I declare
With a smell and a smack and a tang and a crack
I'm as keen as a bee for my share

SINGLE MAN: *(opening his eyes wide, staring at the menu and hitting his forehead with the heel of his left hand)* Oh my goodness. Waiter you're not going to serve me are you? Oh, I'm sorry, I'm so sorry my dear fellow, coming in here, just because I have plenty of money and I was hungry and wanted a meal, how foolish of me. I do apologize, waiter, old boy. I see this is a family restaurant. *(looks around and sees pictures and artifacts on walls, he rises as one leaving)*

WAITER: But what's wrong with us, Sir? We serve very good food, our prices are very competitive. *(aside)* Compared to the Taj Mahal or the White House.

SINGLE MAN: *(standing)* Oh, but you see I'm not eligible – I'm single. Sorry old chum and all that . . .

WAITER: *(relieved)* Oh, I see. But that's all right. Why that's just fine, Sir. That doesn't matter at all.

SINGLE MAN: *(sitting down puzzled)* Really? It doesn't matter?

WAITER: *(wiping the table smugly)* No, No.

SINGLE MAN: But perhaps you don't grasp my full point, dear chap. I'm not a family man, my parents are dead. I've no brothers or sisters - I'm single - unmarried. Surely you can't be thinking of serving me in a family restaurant? Why, I even live on my own, old boy.

WAITER: *(spreading his hands in a gesture of tolerance)* That's all right, Sir, we'll still serve you.

SINGLE MAN: *(severely)* Is the owner or manager aware of this tolerant policy, dear boy?

WAITER: Oh yes Sir, it's just fine with us. I'm part owner.

SINGLE MAN: *(puzzled)* Then why is this place called a family restaurant. Isn't that very misleading?

WAITER: Well Sir, I suppose the word family conjures up pleasant thoughts. It's a nice name - family folks are good souls you know, Sir.

SINGLE MAN: I don't know about that. Ghengis Khan, Winston Churchill, Cesar Borgia and Josef Stalin were all family men, whereas lots of single men like me are perfectly decent souls. Wouldn't you agree, dear chap?

WAITER: Certainly Sir. Family restaurant simply means *(thinks, hesitates, then with sudden light dawning on him)* - we serve families.

The waiter is pleased and beams at understanding the usage.

SINGLE MAN: *(raised eyebrows, enlightened, smiling)* Ah now I see, I see - you serve families.

WAITER: *(laughing and pleased to have made his point)* Yes Sir, we serve families. *(he spreads his hands)* Yes.

SINGLE MAN: *(rubbing his hands together)* Ah, now I see, old chap. Well, good, in that case just serve me up a wife and two kids will you, there's a good fellow. *(sighs)* I'm tired of being single anyhow. *(seriously)* It can be lonely you know - yes, just serve me with a wife and one or two kids - one will do fine.

WAITER: *(confused)* But Sir, I do not mean that we provide families. But *(considers and brightens)* if you bring your own then we'll serve them with a meal. See?

SINGLE MAN: *(sternly)* Look here. This is a family restaurant, right waiter.

WAITER: Yes Sir.

SINGLE MAN: *(adamantly)* Then I want a family. Now are you going to get me a family or are you not?

WAITER: *(looking around, embarrassed)* Shush, quiet, Sir. We can't do that. You need to bring your own family and then we'll serve them.

SINGLE MAN: *(slapping his knee and holding up his right index finger)* Right, that's what I said all along – that's what I said to begin with. Right? You don't want single men here. I have to provide my own family. Isn't that true?

WAITER: *(confused and scratching his head)* Well, I suppose so, Sir.

SINGLE MAN: See. This is discrimination against the Single Man. Why should I have to get my own family when all the worst rogues in the world have got families?

WAITER: Sir! I'm lost.

SINGLE MAN: Very well. So you admit I'm right? You do discriminate against singles, eh? Just as I said to begin with, right? *(Single Man stands up)* I'm afraid I'll have to leave in protest.

> *Waiter bows and throws wide his hands in confusion, shaking his head.*

<u>Curtain</u>

SCENE TWO - FAMILIES ARE GOOD, EH?

Scene: *The same, a few moments later. Single Man is about to leave and has turned away from his table. The waiter has moved to the right of Single Man, between Single Man and the door and is pleading with the customer to reconsider.*

WAITER: Now, Sir, please feel free to leave if you don't like the place or the fare - that is your privilege, but, Sir, I wouldn't want you to leave on a misunderstanding. Please sit down and let me explain. You see, Sir, I'm part-owner of this restaurant and I need the business - you see I've a family to support - I have a wife and three kids too.

SINGLE MAN: *(with interest, sitting down again)* Oh, so you're a family man, old chap. Now I'm beginning to see the picture. That explains a lot.

WAITER: *(pleased)* Yes, Sir. I have children to feed.

SINGLE MAN: *(ironically)* So let them eat here free of charge - what, old boy?

WAITER: *(horrified)* What - at these prices? O, I couldn't afford that Sir.

SINGLE MAN: Ah, so I should pay these prices but not you - because you're a family man, dear chap, eh? And I'm just a victimized, hated, spat upon, loathed single person, eh? I'm to be ripped off and exploited and gouged out from the inmost guts but not you or your nice little family. See what I mean?

WAITER: Dear, dear, do let me explain. It's not discrimination. My family is too poor to eat here and we just call it a family cafe because it seemed like a good healthy image – it's just a wholesome business persona. See Sir?

SINGLE MAN: *(coolly looking at his nails)* Yes my dear chap I do see. *(waiter smiles and fawns and nods)* Yes I do see – it's a healthy image - but me *(suddenly outraged)* I'm single, so I'm unhealthy, is that it? I'm a freak eh? So there's something abnormal about me - is that the way of it dear fellow - because I'm single, I'm an oddity. Yes? Go ahead, be honest, say it, there's something wrong with me – that's it isn't it. Say it. Say it and I'll knock your oafish head off. Go ahead, say so, say I'm a weirdo . . . I dare you.

WAITER: *(horrified)* No, No, Sir. I never thought it for a moment. It's just that "family" seems to mean "good" to a lot of people. Single is good too Sir, of course, naturally -

why my brother Tom is single and he hasn't been in jail for years – he's a fine reformed person.

SINGLE MAN: Ahh! A Jailbird - I knew it, you associate singles with criminals. That's it, now I see it. We're the rejects of society - the castaways of life, marooned on desert islands of social isolation where we will trouble no one's conscience.

He thumps table in despair. Other diners glance up briefly and then return to their meals and silent talk and books. He points a finger of accusation at the waiter.

SINGLE MAN: You, you force me to pay more tax than you do while you squirm out of your fiscal duty just because you have kids, eh? Why should I pay more tax just because you have been improvident and reckless and couldn't care less? Why should I support you and yours, why should you get all the breaks and handouts while all I get is abuse and accusations of being a freaked out whacko eh? *(getting more and more hysterical)*

Oh no, dear boy, so families are good eh, what about the crime families. What about all you married men who started wars and sent out us poor single blokes to fight for you. *(accusingly)*

Oh yes, single is bad, family is good, is it? You family men get all the days off for sick kids. You rob and get caught - you did it to feed your kids. Oh yes. You skipped class in college, didn't do your homework, you avoided the auditor, the health inspector - all because your Ma supposedly died or your granny or your brat was sick. Isn't that the truth?

How many Ma's or Granmas or brats have you had die to cover up and help you hide from your blunders? You hide behind your family, don't you and so, naturally, family is a good image you say - I think it's a terrible word.

WAITER: *(looking around in fear - at his wits end to placate Single Man)* Well, there's good families and bad families but look, what you say has made me think - maybe you're right – "family" can be taken either way, so maybe we'll change the name of the cafe to say, healthy or health food or goodies - how about that – we'll leave out the word "family." How about that Sir?

SINGLE MAN: *(horrified and pointing at waiter)* Oh so you'll change the name, dear boy, will you? Leave out the word "family," eh?

Waiter nods happily

SINGLE MAN: So that's it - change the mere name and catch out people like me unawares, eh? Entrap us, mislead us, get us in here on false pretenses and then insult us and rip us off - oh, no, oh no Sir - never - never - never will I bow to that kind of deceit and decrepit deception – I'll expose you as a true family eatery at heart. I'll never let you get away with it. I'll write to the world press. I'll show you up for what you really are *(slowly and sinisterly pointing a finger at the waiter)* - a family man.

WAITER: So, so, I'll not change the name - if it makes you happy. I'll keep the name "family." All right, all right. "Family restaurant."

SINGLE MAN: *(triumphantly)* I knew it. Familyism survives after all. I can see the headlines. Familyism wins again. Oh, it's too terrible.

He buries his head in his hands and begins to sob and thump the table.

SINGLE MAN: Oh its too much. Familyism rules the waves - boo hoo hoo.

He sobs. Waiter gasps, raises his head and hands in despair as other customers look slightly embarrassed and exchange odd glances.

WAITER: Cheer up, Sir. This is just a good old fashioned caf. You can even have a fish and chips here.

Sings. **FISH AND CHIPS**

Sung: Fast

VERSE 1 AND REFRAIN:

s d - d m s d^1 t
O I'll have some fish and chips please
d^1 r^1 l - l - l - l
If that's all right with you
f r - r - r f t - t - t
Not too much grease - some mushy peas
l s s s - f m
And salt and vinegar too
s d - d m - s d^1 - d^1 t
No more the dainty dinner do
d^1 r^1 l - l - l - l
No more them dunking dips
l s s - s s - t t l
I say if it's all right with you
s - s s f r d
I'll have some fish and chips

VERSE 1 AND REFRAIN:

O I'll have some fish and chips please
If that's all right with you
Not too much grease - some mushy peas
And salt and vinegar too
No more the dainty dinner do
No more them dunking dips
I say if it's all right with you
I'll have some fish and chips

VERSE 2:
Now the Admiral was in the pink
His ships were spiffy clean
Your Majesty what do you think?
He asks the blooming Queen
Says the Queen I absolutely love
This fleet of men and ships
The only thing they need more of
Is good old fish and chips

VERSE 3:
Well my Uncle Ray drops dead one day
We lay him down in flowers
Then we start a party right away
To brighten those sad hours
Ahh . . suddenly he bolts upright
And fear and terror grips . . .
We ask, What brought you back? He cried
I smell some fish and chips

VERSE 4:
See I knew a glamour girl I say
As pretty as the moon
Says she, Come visit me some day
So I showed up right soon
She asked, What would you like to do?
And smiled those lovely lips
I said, If it's all right with you
We'll have some fish and chips

Curtain

SCENE THREE – BUT WIVES AND KIDS ARE REAL

Scene: The same, a few moments later. Single Man is still sobbing, but less volubly. Waiter pats Single Man on the shoulder and Single Man begins to dry his tears.

WAITER: There, there, Sir - Cheer up. Tell you what, you can have anything, anything in the house, Sir, at half price. *(he points to items on the menu)*

SINGLE MAN: *(drying up, somewhat, but still sniveling)* Oh, it's so tough being single - no grandchildren to play with, no measles to get the victory over, no summer camps to watch the dear little kids at. No school events to thrill one - see what I mean dear fellow? No grandpa to fall down my stairs. No brother to kick me . . .

WAITER: *(sympathetically)* I know Sir. No little girls with little curls, no little boys with little toys - but *(cheering up)* that's why I'm offering you anything in the house at half-price - *(aside to audience)* the prices are already double what they should be - *(to Single Man)* that's to compensate you for being caught out in a family café.

Waiter nods and winks at audience.

WAITER: There, there.

Waiter pats Single Man on shoulder.

SINGLE MAN: *(naively)* Half-price, old boy. That's jolly decent of you and all that, old chap.

Single Man begins to study the menu but his eyes slowly drift above it to the family in the left-back corner of stage where the large wife and kids still tend to hide the small father. Single Man's eyes focus on this family group.

Waiter, suspecting something strange, based on his immediate experience of Single Man, covers his eyes and groans.

WAITER: Oh, no, no, please no.

SINGLE MAN: Yes, I need a wife and family. How much is that *(pointing to corner family group)* wife and family over there?

WAITER: *(dusting table furiously in nervous agitation)* How much? But Sir, they're not for sale. I can't just sell them to you, Sir. They're not mine!

SINGLE MAN: No – they're mine from now on - *(raising his voice and pointing to the family group)* Hey you, wife and children, I'll have you, if you don't mind, at half price too.

WIFE: *(standing up and shielding her husband)* What on earth do you mean?

SINGLE MAN: I'm tired of being single - I just want to buy you all as my wife and children since the waiter here has put you on offer, O.K?

The small husband comes out from behind his wife and marches towards the door (exit right) past the waiter and Single Man, beckoning his wife and children after him. All march out as the lady diner, middle-stage, looks concerned and surprised.

SMALL HUSBAND: How dare you, young feller, these are my wife and kids and not for sale, Sir.

***The family group march offstage** in line behind the small husband, heads in air, in disdain.*

SINGLE MAN: *(to husband)* I beg your pardon. I didn't see you, Sir!

SMALL HUSBAND: So I'm a dwarf, am I? Yes?

WAITER: *(calling after the departing group)* But you haven't paid Sir.

LARGE WIFE: *(departing)* After that insult - you should pay us!

The family all leave, heads in air.

Waiter drops his towel in despair and staggers weakly against a table, one hand on his head, his mouth open, his other hand on the table to steady himself and preventing him from fainting.

SINGLE MAN: *(pointing to middle-aged, well dressed diner in center stage)* Can I have that one instead? At half-price?

WAITER: *(gasping)* But she's a respectable lady, Sir.

The middle-aged lady is horrified at these remarks and begins to gather together her belongings and put on her hat and coat as these remarks continue loudly, between Waiter and Single Man.

SINGLE MAN: Of course, she's a respectable lady. It was you who put her on sale at half-price, not me. I can see she's a respectable lady - what other kind of wife do you think I would want, old fellow, eh? Do I look like a chap who would want to marry a brazen hussy, a painted floozy, a trollopy tart, a shameless, sleazy slum-slut - for a wife? So that is what you think of me, eh? So . . you stand there accusing me of being a low class, slam, ram, bam slimy slob with no discretion or civilized discrimination. Do you; oh, really? *(He clasps and unclasps his hands hysterically)*

(pushing back his sleeve aggressively and standing up) Am I like that, Waiter, Old Boy, am I?

WAITER: *(backing away)* Oh dear no, no, no, Sir. It's just the time, the place, the occasion - is not appropriate. You know Sir – it's nothing personal against you, Sir, but the lady is really quite young, barely middle-aged, genteel and beautiful.

SINGLE MAN: Ah, now I understand. You think that I'm an impoverished, penniless, desperate and despicable starveling who would grasp at the bones of any lean cadaver of marital rejection. So I'm the one who would seize any scraggy bag of withered bones, a dried-up immolated hag, a skinny shriveled-up old crone moaning and groaning and creaking and squeaking like a wooden floor or door - a scrawny mummy - you think I deserve a wife like that - that - THAT'S what you're saying, isn't it? Admit it? You think this lady is too good for me, eh?

WAITER: I never even thought of such a vile thing, Sir. My mind is set on a very simple business matter, I assure you, my dear Sir.

SINGLE MAN: And just what is that "simple business matter," my good fellow?

WAITER: *(naively)* Why, food for money, Sir. Just that, a restaurant, an eatery, food for money. Simple - see? *(Waiter spreads his hands)*

SINGLE MAN: *(calming down)* Oh, I see, quite well, old boy. Well, you made the offer you know. Remember? Anything in the house - half-price and all that. So, *(eagerly)* can I have her then?

Lady, head high, begins to walk past the two disputants in disgust.

Oh, lady, come back, on second thoughts I'll pay full price for you as a wife.

WAITER: *(to Single Man)* Oh, but I meant food and drink only. *(to Lady who is walking out)* But Ma'am, your check!

LADY: *(stomping towards exit, right-stage)* Check? That's a joke - check him out *(motions to Single Man)* He's the freako who needs it!

Lady leaves right.

WAITER: *(calling after her)* Yes, Ma'am, I agree.

SINGLE MAN: Oh do you indeed - so I'm a kinko? Am I? I knew that was what you were trying to say all along. How dare you! Family

Restaurant indeed. I'll never set foot in another brat-based cafe in my life.

Single Man stomps out, stage right.

WAITER: Oh, thank you Sir. I'll hold you to that promise.

Waiter looks around in distress at the empty dining room, sighs, sobs, wipes his eyes with his left hand and waves his right hand outwards in a gesture of despair.

WAITER: *(holding both his hands out towards the audience)* Now, how am I going to feed my wife and children? Oh my poor family.

FINALE: *To end the show, all three songs should now be sung in the order of their appearance.*

Curtain

END OF PLAYSCRIPT

THE VIEWING OF AUNTIE AGATHA

A Short Story and a Two-Act Play

The Story

Aunt Agatha was a white-haired, elderly lady. She lived for ninety-nine years and then one day she died.

Aunt Agatha was laid out in her coffin in the parlor of her home. She wore a white shroud; her hands were folded across her chest. The coffin was tilted upwards on trestles for a last viewing by her relatives. Also on trestles and raised up was a large aspidistra in a gold and silver pot.

The rest of the room was lined with regular living room furniture - such as dining table, chairs, sofas, rocking chair, cabinet, piano, desk-bureau and fireplace with mantle. There were some sandwiches and drinks on the table, in expectation of visitors.

The walls of the parlor were decorated with old-fashioned pictures and the floor was covered with navy colored square patterned vinyl with one or two patterned rugs on top.

Along the left wall of the parlor was an open doorway leading to the kitchen. In all, a comfortable parlor with oldish furniture that contrasted with the large flashy aspidistra in the gold and silver pot close to the wall. It was a mundane scene that could be almost anywhere in the world.

The doorbell rang, announcing the arrival of the first of many expected guests. The younger sister of the deceased, Kate, was mid-aged, and wore a white blouse, piled-up hair and long black skirt. Briskly she crossed the floor, opened the door and admitted Uncle Fred the undertaker. He was an elderly man dressed in an old fashioned gentlemanly style. Hat, gloves, dark formal clothes, and black shoes, white shirt, black tie. Fred was shaky and trembling in voice and gesture, with age and infirmity. He entered, still holding the door open, hands on chest, with gravity.

He approached the coffin, rubbed his hands together and then looked around as one satisfied with his handiwork in setting up the display containing Auntie Agatha.

"Ah, Sister Kate," he said, "How do you like my handiwork? I sent her here earlier you know." He looked around disappointed at the furniture but brightened when he saw the aspidistra.

Kate respectfully addressed the undertaker, looking sadly at the coffin, "I know, Uncle Fred. You did a good job in setting her up. She's very like herself, so she is."

Fred answered her keenly, "Aye - Very lifelike, that's true. I've never seen her look better. She glows with brightness and beauty. Aye, that last illness of hers must have done her a world of good."

Kate was startled and asked querulously, "But she's dead. Isn't she?"

"Of course," agreed Fred, "but I mean a world of good in her appearance, although we morticians add a little makeup too - so maybe I should take the credit. But sometimes illness makes one look better." He tapped his midriff, "Reduces weight perhaps."

Kate looked down at her own tummy, "Oh yes, I wish I could take sick at times. It must be very good for one's health."

Fred nodded and formally agreed. "The dear departed being my favorite aunt, I am, of course, offering the funeral services, including dressing and display that you see here - entirely free of charge - a small service to our family . . ."

"We're all very grateful." Kate wept slightly.

Uncle Fred looked around and shook his head in disappointment, "Poor Auntie Agatha would not have left anywhere near as much as it would have taken to employ our services. These few sticks of furniture - pathetic. Ah, it is so sad to see that after a lifetime of hard and faithful work, the poor departed leaves only a few sticks - none of which I am personally interested in, I may say."

Kate subtly positioned herself between Fred and the aspidistra. She was slightly protective.

Noticing this, Fred looked around her at the aspidistra and then continued carefully, "Of course, my only aim is for the good of the community as a whole. Perhaps some small thing of no value to enhance the funeral chapel and to enrich the lives of the bereaved widows and orphans who go there to weep and mourn their dear departed. Ah, yes, some little brightening token to cheer them up. Perhaps I might be constrained upon to accept some such . . ."

He looked enviously at the aspidistra. "A small toy, some bauble, valueless in itself but bringing joy to the heart of the poor, the stricken, the mournful."

Kate nodded and answered eagerly, "You mean like balloons. Yes . . . I'm sure . . ."

The undertaker was outraged, "What do you mean, Sister Kate, by 'balloons'? Balloons, Ma'am?" He thundered. "What of balloons?"

Kate squirmed uncomfortably and nodded innocently, "Little red and blue and green plastic bags of air to cheer up the orphans. Yes?"

Fred began to examine the aspidistra pot, picking at it carefully, "How dare you, Ma'am! How dare you insult those poor little orphans. Whoever heard of balloons at a funeral service? Why do you think the bereaved attend - to celebrate? Who? Who Ma'am, would want to celebrate the passing of a relative? . . Who? Who? Answer me, who?"

Kate was still evasive, "Well, it would depend on the relative, wouldn't it Uncle Fred? What about the piano? I'm sure no one would object to your taking the old - I mean the genuine antique - piano?"

Fred sighed, "No, we already have two pianos. No, I wouldn't want anything as valuable as that - just that silly aspidistra would cheer up the orphans and widows so well . . ."

Kate stamped her foot angrily, "Over my dead body! Oh, I beg your pardon Auntie - no offence intended." She addressed Fred bluntly and blurted out, "You can't have it. O.K?"

Fred scratched his chin and asked sharply, "And why not? What if Auntie Agatha wanted me to have it? The will has not been read, has it? You didn't see the will did you?"

"No, I didn't," admitted Kate. "But I know for a fact that Auntie Agatha did not want you to have it. I was her secretary - voluntary, of course - for her last years."

Fred frowned in disappointment, "Hmm, ah, now I see. She didn't like me, did she? So why am I burying her free, eh? I wonder?"

Then Kate asked evasively, "Who said she didn't like you? She liked you a lot. I only said . . ."

"I know what you said but I also know what Auntie Agatha thought about me."

"How could you?"

Fred looked at Kate knowingly, "Because secretaries are like dogs."

"What?" asked Kate, confused.

Fred explained, "Yes, dogs always give their owners away. The dog barks and snarls when you approach – it's only acting out the sneers and groans and stiffness it picks up from its owner when he sees you coming. It doesn't have the sophistication to fake a liking for you. Yes, secretaries are the same. The subtle clues of dislike, disdain, distrust of me that you picked up from Auntie Agatha - all came out in your big ugly clock when I used to visit you and Auntie Agatha - your clock certainly tells the time – I'll say that for you."

Kate smiled weakly, "It's not true. I'm just downcast at dear Auntie's death."

"Don't fool me," said Fred, "You were always frowning and tense every time I ever visited dear old Auntie Agatha." He paused and reconsidered, "Well, anyhow, if the rest of the family agree that I should have a small reward, it's very likely that you'll agree too. After all, it's only to brighten things up for the widows and orphans in my chapel of remembrance."

"Why not charge them a little less, then they'll be really grateful?" said Kate sarcastically.

Kate's sarcasm began to annoy Fred. "Oh dear, this is too much for me," he said "I wish I was a poor gravedigger again, like in the good old days before the war."

Fred drew himself up to his full height with dignity, opened his mouth as if to say something more, was lost for words, shook his head in disgust and proceeded to examine the gold pot holding the aspidistra.

Fred was very pleased with his examination of the pot, "Yes, very nice, solid gold with inlaid silver - very nice indeed . . . Just right for the First Chapel of Rest."

Kate folded her arms and stamped her foot in disdain.

Kate continued on in her sarcastic mood. "Why are chapels and churches always being set against each other like racing greyhounds, first, second, third Baptist or Presbyterian. There must be better or more spiritual ways to distinguish one church from another. It's so childish. It's like kids saying, me, me, I was first."

She stuck her tongue out and put her fingers in her ears. Kate went on, "Ya, ya, ya. Boo, boo, boo. Boo, boo, boo. Boo, boo, boo. Hiss, hiss, hiss. Ya, ya, ya. We were here first. We were here first. We were here first. Why not, not you? How did you miss? Ha, ha, ha."

This made Fred feel rather smug and he replied, "Well, it's nice to be a winner, like First Chapel of Rest."

Kate sarcasticated, "Oh, yes, you hardly ever hear of a fourth or fifth church or a 22nd one. Only the three top medal winners, but especially number one." She cocked her head quizzically at Fred.

Fred placed his hands on hips and glared back at Kate. Then they both stuck their fingers in their ears and put out their tongues at each other.

Kate and Fred continued making negative gestures at each other. Kate was shaking fists, Fred was wagging his index finger. Both were puffing and blowing. They turned their backs to each other, as there was a knock on the door. As Kate opened the door, Fred turned again to examine the aspidistra.

The new caller was cousin Charlie, a law officer, who saluted all and sundry in a somewhat vacant manner.

Officer Charlie wagged his finger in admonishment at Kate, "I've warned you many times - not to open the door like that without finding out who is outside."

Kate protested naively, "But if I hadn't opened the door Charlie, how could you have come in?"

"But how did you know it was me?" asked Charlie severely.

Kate replied primly, "Well, I was right, wasn't I?"

Charlie took a deep breath and replied, slowly, syllable by syllable. "Look, everybody who was ever murdered by an intruder had been right in opening doors and letting people in - on every occasion in their life except the last one. See?" Then reverting to normal speech, Charlie continued, "Now, tell me, why did you open the door - just like that?"

Kate answered self-righteously, "Charlie, it was you who knocked the door. Now . . you know you did. Isn't that true?"

Then addressing Fred, "Charlie knocked, didn't he?"

Fred nodded but was still preoccupied with examining the pot of gold.

Officer Charlie shook his head in officious disdain and spoke up in an outraged tone, "Doors are meant to keep people out not to let people in. If we just wanted to let people in we could live outdoors and provide a lawn for our visitors. Heck no. Doors are meant to keep out humans and dogs. See . . an open door is a contradiction in terms, a paradox, an oxymoron and a very dangerous incongruity. Ahem . . a car that does not drive, a plane that doesn't fly is all the same as a door that does not stay closed. Hmm . . see? Anyone who opens a door just because someone knocks it, doesn't need a door, doesn't deserve a door. Why not just leave a hole in the wall? Or live in a cave?"

Kate responded perkily, "But, Cousin Charlie, that way it would get cold in here. And besides, anyone could just walk in through a hole in the wall. So don't be silly."

Charlie appeared somewhat dazed by Kate's logic. "Well, that's exactly what I mean, anyone could just walk in if you open the door just because someone knocks."

Kate shook her head, "Oh no they couldn't, Charlie."

"And why not, Kate?"

Kate perked up triumphantly, "Because I closed it immediately after you came in. And besides, you wouldn't let them, would you Charlie?"

Charlie was still slightly dazed, "Who? Me?"

Kate answered smugly, "Yes, you wouldn't let them."

"Let them what?" answered Charlie.

"Let just anyone walk in, would you, Charlie?"

Charlie blinked uncertainly, "Well . . no . . ."

"See! You're a policeman, aren't you?"

Charlie was confused but proud, "Oh, yes. Yes, of course." He straightened his shoulders. "Sure, sure, I'm a policeman. I just want you to be safe."

"Well then, what have I got to worry about?" asked Kate.

But Charlie was still confused, "O, I see. You mean you're safe on this occasion?"

Kate smiled, "Exactly, Charlie. That's what I've been trying to say to you."

Charlie passed his open palms across his eyes - shook his head to clear his thinking and then walked over reverently to view Auntie Agatha.

He murmured, in admiration, "Ah, what a fine figure of a gentlewoman, my own dear departed Aunt Agatha." He began to look more closely at Aunt Agatha. "Hmm, who trussed her up like this? I suppose it was you, Fred? Is this kidnapping, I wonder?" Charlie scratched his head, quizzically.

Fred the undertaker was outraged, "Kidnapping? What do you mean? The deceased has to be strapped in, in case she falls out."

Charlie snorted, "How could she? She's dead, isn't she?"

Fred nodded seriously, "Oh, she's dead all right. But what if someone slipped while carrying the coffin?"

It was Charlie's turn now to become sarcastic, "Oh, I see. I thought perhaps you were afraid she might escape."

Fred shook his head solemnly, "Oh no. There's no chance of that."

Charlie shook his head, "I know. I know. Only kidding, Fred. Why are people so humorless on these occasions? Once you fellows get your hands on a body, it's all up, isn't it? I mean, all down, you know - ha, ha. No jail breaks from you lot eh? So everyone sits around with faces as long as a gravedigger's spade. Come on, cheer up."

Fred the undertaker became plaintive and answered, "Oh dear. I wish I was a poor gravedigger again, just like in the good old days before the war. This is much too much for me."

Fred looked pained but smiled slightly. Charlie began to notice and take an interest in the gold-potted aspidistra. He looked it over. At this point there was another knock on the door and Officer Charlie held up his hand in a gesture of caution directed at Kate.

"Ah, ah, ah – remember Kate?"

Fred told Charlie, "You're paranoid."

Charlie quipped back at Fred, "You'd be insane not to be paranoid in this life."

But Kate opened the door, asking, "Who's there?"

A voice replied, "Your niece, Gypsy Posey."

No sooner had she spoken than Gypsy Posey stepped inside. She was a fortuneteller in colorful formal dress with long black hair tied back, and deep dark eyes.

She waved her hand at the others, "Good luck to all here." She approached the coffin and looked long and hard at Auntie Agatha. "May everyone here enjoy long life and happiness! Oh, I beg your pardon, Auntie Agatha. No offence intended." She dabbed her eyes. "Oh, it was so unexpected and sudden."

Fred the undertaker remarked cynically, rolling his eyes, "Well, of course, she was 99 and suffered from a bad heart - so it shouldn't have been all that unexpected. Ah, if only people would look ahead a little and plot their plots."

Gypsy Posey brightened, "Pay you up front, you mean. Yes, that's what I tell them. Look ahead -

through the tea leaves. It's worth the small fee I charge."

Fred continued mournfully, "Well, we all should know that we can't last forever. A little financial planning for the planting and her funeral could have been paid for in advance - as it is, I am donating all the funeral services, including the dressing of the corpse as you see." He pointed to Auntie Agatha and then linked his hands together, primly in front of his chest. "And all I am asking in return, dear Niece Gypsy, if you all approve, is for this little old aspidistra to grace my chapel."

The gypsy looked with sudden interest at the plant as Officer Charlie was still examining the gold pot.

"Who assayed this gold?" asked Charlie.

Gypsy Posey was astonished. "Gold? Real gold?" the gypsy cried out. "Oh, dear Aunt Aggie had such good taste. She was such a wonderful person."

Fred looked far into the sky and became philosophical, "Yes, but all good things must pass away. Just like the bad things of life. Alas, where are the ladies of days gone?"

Kate replied, "Ask a theologian."

Charlie responded, "Well don't look at me. Only my boss calls me names - that way I get paid for it. See?"

Fred tried to calm things down, "Of course, it must be a misunderstanding."

Gypsy Posey began a more careful examination of the aspidistra. "This would be ideal for my consulting room."

Officer Charlie looked cynically at the gypsy, "With the kind of clients you have, that thing would be gone the first time you left the room. It would look much nicer and be a lot safer on my porch."

Gypsy Posey responded, "O, but I never leave my clients alone in the room. What do you take me for? It's a professional office - not a hotel, you know."

Officer Charlie shook his head in horror, "I'm glad to hear it. Just how exactly would you describe your practice? Witchcraft? Voodoo? Séance? Mumbo Jumbo?"

"No, no. You know perfectly well that I'm merely a fortuneteller."

"Aha, a crystal ball gazer eh? That's what I suspected, that's what I heard. Charging people for telling fortunes with cards, tea leaves or crystals is against the law around here."

The gypsy shook her head in disgust at this idea, "Oh, everything is against the law nowadays. There's laws against guns, laws against every known trade and profession and business unless you have a license, laws against using your house for a business, laws against drugs and even alcohol in times and places and every single one of your silly laws is just there to protect vested interests and keep the newcomers from making a living."

Officer Charlie began to laugh, "Really? First I heard of it. So who are the insider fortunetellers I'm protecting? Eh?"

Gypsy Posey answered quickly, "Oh, you don't know? The religion industry, of course, meteorologists, psychologists, psychiatrists, financial advisers and economists. There are plenty of them and they foretell it all wrong just as often as I do. If I had a Ph.D. in Economics, I could fortunetell to my heart's content, get it wrong every time and still make a pretty penny. All right?"

Charlie responded defensively, "Well, at least economists can make an educated guess. You can't!"

The gypsy replied somewhat tearfully, "So I should use math models to base my false predictions on - then I'd still be wrong, dead wrong but on the right side of the law, eh? It seems to me that most of your laws are there merely to prevent the have-nots from becoming haves. Nothing against the economist who is lying but all against a poor lady fortuneteller who only tries to make people happy. All your laws do is keep the hungry outsiders out and keep the greedy insiders in. Greed, you know, is the root of all evil according to the good book."

Charlie shrugged his shoulders and looked mystified as Kate spoke up.

"I think you're both in the wrong. This aspidistra should go to me as a reward for my secretarial - part-time but voluntary - services to Auntie Agatha for so many months before her beloved departure."

Fred replied coolly, "You mean the departure of the beloved. Look, you all want the aspidistra for yourselves or your homes. But I would agree to resolve this stalemate, this potential family row. Believe me, I am prepared to resolve this dispute, act as a good Samaritan - a peacemaker - not, not I say by taking this plant for myself but rather by mediating ."

"Yes, how?" asked the others in unison.

The undertaker replied, "Well, acting purely for the public good." He smiled hollowly. "And without serving any personal motive - it could be placed in the First Chapel of Rest . . . "

Charlie added in a cold tone, sitting down, "As a public service?"

Gypsy Posey spoke up with raised eyebrows. "Not to enhance your private business as an undertaker?"

Kate added sarcastically, "Just to cheer up the orphans?"

Fred nodded eagerly, unaware of the sarcasm, "Right, exactly."

Gypsy Posey suggested, "I know something else you could do for the orphans."

Fred bowed and smiled, "Yes, dear niece, what is that?"

The gypsy replied coldly, "Stop ripping them off, so that they wouldn't have to spend half their lives saving up just to end up dead and dumped in your rubbish heap for dead bodies. Your human garbage pile with flowers on top."

All three began to glare in an unfriendly way at Uncle Fred. The undertaker looked miserable and moaned, "Oh, I used to be so happy as a young and carefree and innocent gravedigger, in the good old days before the war. The war ruined everything. People just aren't the same. I remember the time when . . ." He pointed accusingly at Officer Charlie, "People didn't even bother to lock their doors, never mind worry about opening them. Before you cops got your computers, cars, spy systems and started taping everyone. For all your spying and taping, crime has gone through the roof."

Officer Charlie shrugged, "What am I supposed to do about it?"

Fred answered, "Do what you all did before - when crime was low. . ."

"What's that?" asked Charlie.

"Simple," said Fred, "Get back on the street, on the beat, on your feet."

All the mourning relatives of Aunt Agatha were standing around looking at each other in a mystified and awkward manner. It was gradually beginning to dawn on them that no one person could be the winner and that some sort of compromise was becoming a more acceptable idea. They tried hard to think of a more friendly and more productive approach except that all four relatives were now standing looking at the aspidistra set in its golden pot. The challenge now was to compromise and share.

The gypsy was the first to try to break the ice, "Look, it's so silly arguing about who gets the aspidistra. When the executor, nephew Twoomey, reads the will he'll make sure it goes to the one that Auntie Agatha willed it to. Now the only way around that is if we can all agree."

Officer Charlie rubbed his hands enthusiastically, "That's right, we can all agree on what to do with our own property."

Uncle Fred concurred, "So let's agree on something . . but what?"

Kate tentatively suggested, "Well, the aspidistra with its gold pot is very valuable. There's no doubt about that. Why Auntie Agatha just almost worshipped it - she said it was the culmination of her life's work - she wouldn't even let me water it - she doted on it. So, since it's worth a lot, why don't we agree to sell it and share out the profits - no matter who gets it. Now, if Granma Pegg - she should be along soon - agrees, we'll split it five ways – isn't that fair?"

The undertaker, Fred, was rather reluctant but muttered, "I suppose so."

Gypsy Posey was much more keen, "Of course . . it's fair. That gold pot is an antique. It could be worth a fortune. Now 20% of 100,000 is 20,000 – that's better than a poke in the eye with a sharp stick."

Officer Charlie nodded in agreement.

The gypsy summed it all up, "Right. Let's all shake on it and when Gran Pegg comes let's all act real casual and not act like it's worth a whole lot so that she'll agree. After all, if one person contested us on behalf of the will, it could cost us a pretty penny in legal fees."

They all shook hands and smiled and agreed. Pleased with the deal, Uncle Fred posed beside the coffin, placed one hand on the coffin and the other on his lapel while the others stood by and listened politely, smiling cheerfully and nodding to each other in appreciation of his offering.

"Yes," said Fred. "Let's look on the bright side - every cloud has a silver lining."

Kate agreed, "Oh, what a wonderful original thought!"

Uncle Fred gazed into the distance, speaking loudly and poetically, "Alas we pass like flotsam on the shores of life."

All agreed tearfully.

Uncle Fred pointed to imaginary driftwood. "Longfeller, my dear Sister Kate, ah . . Longfeller."

Kate said, "O do invite him in, Fred, all mourners are welcome, no matter how tall." She sniffed and dabbed her nose as Uncle Fred opened the door and looked out, quite mystified, shrugged and declared, "There's no one there."

Kate, also mystified, replied dimly and shakily, "I thought you said there was a skinny chap outside."

Confused, Uncle Fred closed the door, "Dear me, no. No, no. A misunderstanding, my dear Sister Kate. I thought I was quoting Longfellow but perhaps it was Yeats."

Kate tried to change the subject by lifting a small tray of goodies and passing it to Uncle Fred and the others while smiling sweetly. "Oh yes, we've plenty of eats - have a salad sandwich."

Fred shook his head sadly, "No thanks. You must have misunderstood. No, I'm trying to lose weight. Food is bad for you. Auntie Agatha ate and ate all of her life and just look what it did to her at the end."

Gypsy Posey pointed to the coffin, "But everyone ends up like this."

Fred continued fearfully, "Exactly and everyone eats, don't they? Eating is a much overrated pastime, Ma'am." He shook his head. "It overtaxes the system, yes Ma'am."

But the others ate and drank a little, still nodding politely to each other. There was a knock on the door. Kate approached the door sedately, smiling at Cousin Charlie, who nodded approvingly.

Kate continued to look at Officer Charlie, calling out loudly, "Who's there?"

A voice answered from the other side of the door, "Granny Pegg."

Charlie called out to his fellow mourners, "Hold on. Just a minute. Look! Granny Pegg is a tough old schoolmarm. Once she makes up her mind about anything – she'll never change it. Let's make sure we do a good job of persuading her on what we're all agreed upon." Charlie lowered his voice as the others all nodded in agreement.

Charlie continued quietly, "So let's all sit down and look real casual and pay no special attention to that aspidistra. It's of no account - get it?"

The others agreed and sat down with their drinks and sandwiches, posing casually and politely.

"I'll give her some soft soap about the teaching profession. Then we can casually mention that we've agreed to share everything equally. Get it?" whispered Charlie.

Charlie nodded to Kate, who opened the door and admitted Granny Pegg who was severely dressed in tweed costume, strong flat walking shoes, large old fashioned hat and scarf. She was quite elderly. She nodded to the family members who nodded back, dabbing their eyes and sniffing.

The old granny greeted the mourners, "Good afternoon, Charlie, Fred, Gypsy and dear Kate."

Kate embraced her tearfully and kissed her. The others, while sniffing occasionally, made deliberate attempts to be casual. Crossing legs. Looking at ceiling. Much shaking of heads, sighing and polishing of fingernails on clothes.

Granny Pegg was a stern and aggressive, old lady. All her actions and words made it clear that she was decisive, no nonsense, loud and sure of herself. She approached the coffin and looked at Auntie Agatha as Charlie recited. "I appreciate what you're doing Granny Pegg, trying to blow away cobwebs of ignorance, smarten up young people and straighten out their ideas on goodness and helping their neighbor. The golden rule and all that, yessir Gran.

Greed is bad enough but dumbness and ignorance make this poor life even more of a misery. A good schoolteacher does a real good job."

"Oh, I just loved all my schoolteachers," agreed Kate. "They were so kind to me, I never learned hardly anything at all - I was so happy."

Charlie nodded, "I can believe that. But, see, it's like this, a savvy stockbroker or a smart-aleck lawyer doesn't need to rip you off. He can make heap plenty green stuff just doing his regular thing. Dumb money advisers and numbskull attorneys, dunce real estate agents and the like are too stupid and incompetent to make money except by cheating you. Same with honest, I mean honest-to-goodness thieves - a smart housebreaker cum burglar will make sure, by checking around, whether there is someone at home. A dumb thief will knock on the front door only, get no reply and just bust in. Then lo and behold, the owner is there at the back, sleeping or deaf or just not answering the door and next thing you know there's a confrontation and the house owner maybe gets killed."

"But Charlie, you said not to answer the door just a little while ago. You said . . . Didn't he Fred?"

Fred agreed. "Yes you did . . . You said, Never answer the door. We heard you distinctly. Didn't we?"

The others nodded. But Charlie disagreed stiffly, "Not at all - I said nothing of the kind - always answer, speak to the door, some thief could be testing to see if there's anyone at home. See? What I said was

- do not open the door. Anyhow, Granny Pegg, I appreciate you spreading knowledge, helping kids to wise-up, teaching morals is all great work. Dumbness plus ignorance is a bad combination. Yes, Granny Pegg, teaching is one necessary and one honorable profession. I'm sure I speak for the whole family and the entire neighborhood when I say . . ."

But Pegg was too distressed to think about the teaching profession. She drew close to Aunt Agatha's coffin and examined her closely. "How could anyone die who looks so well? What a fine head of hair. Are you sure that she got proper medical treatment?"

"Oh, yes Granny," replied Kate. "In fact she had a specialist."

Pegg became immediately suspicious, "What kind of specialist?"

Kate was mystified, looked at the others in puzzlement and after the others shook their heads she brightened up, "Well, you got me there. What kind of specialist? But I do know that she had a specialist. Oh, I think he was a heart specialist - yes, a cardiologist. Yes, a cardio - or was it a gerontologist - Oh, well, it was some kind of an 'ologist' anyway."

Pegg pulled at her lips and considered the matter in some depth. She began to think of the various deceased she had known. "Some folks know when they're about to go and some folks don't. The one sort lives about as long as the other. A specialist only tells you the bad news - he doesn't know enough to save you from it. Ah, yes. All they know is their own specialty. Did anyone ever visit a specialist who didn't need that specialist?"

The mourners became glum, looked blank and shrugged, as old Pegg continued, "I'm asking a serious question. Did anyone not need one who ever visited one? Did anyone ever visit any eye specialist and the eye specialist tell them - Oh, you don't need an eye specialist, you need a nerve or a psychology or a back pain specialist. Since I can't help there will be no fee. What rubbish! Specialists all believe they can cure anything – they're quacks.

"No wonder poor Aunt Agatha succumbed to neglect and misunderstanding and physicians. Tragic. Poor lady. Bah! Specialists. I'm asking a serious question since I'm now entering the second half of my life when advancing years take their toll."

Gypsy looked puzzled and counted her fingers and raised her eyebrows and mumbled to herself, "What's she mean - now entering the second half of her life? How long does she think she's going to live? To be a hundred and sixty?"

She shrugged as Pegg went on, "Bah, doctors. A doctor is the last person you need - the very last." Pegg nodded significantly to herself.

But Kate was a little disturbed and muttered, "No. That's a cruel thing to say."

"No? Well, very well, I take that back - AN UNDERTAKER is the very last person you need. A doctor is the second . . ah, the next to last person you need," Pegg amended but Kate was not to be deflected from her train of thought.

"Now Granny Pegg, you're saying that specialist doctors are money grabbers who'll sell you any old trashy treatment. The doctors that I know are there to help whether they make money or not."

Pegg rejected this idea completely, "Altruism - philanthropy - do goodism - whatever you want to call it, is like the ghost and the vampire and the English Constitution. Libraries of books, professors, degrees, schools, whole industries have flourished on it but when you want to see it, it can't be found. Seems like it doesn't even exist. Taint there."

Pegg developed a sudden interest in the aspidistra and cried out, "But this does exist and is very, very interesting. Hmm. That would be nice for my schoolroom - to educate the children on tropical plants, hmm. I wonder to whom Aunt Agatha left this fine specimen?"

Charlie answered, struggling to remain casual, "Well, Granny, it doesn't matter."

Pegg contradicted him, "Of course it does. What do you mean?"

Eagerly, the gypsy chipped in, "Charlie means that since there is no great value in anything and since Auntie Agatha was known to be an eccentric old dear, we're agreed not to go by the literal terms of the will and . . well . . ." She finished, suddenly and sharply, "to share everything equally."

Fred nodded, "Yes, sell it all and divide the proceeds equally - if that's all right with you. You see there's no one thing of any particular value."

Pegg answered somewhat sharply, "Oh good, good. I'm glad to hear that."

Kate was relieved, "So you agree Pegg."

But Pegg was not to be so easily deterred, "Don't be ridiculous. Of course I don't agree. When have I ever agreed to anything in my entire life? When? Tell me, when?"

She glared at the others as gypsy agreed despondently, "No, you're not known for agreeableness - but WE are all agreed."

Old Pegg was pleased at this remark which acknowledged her obnoxiousness, "Well that is nice for you. But I am glad to hear, as I said, that there's nothing of any particular value - for I intend to take the plant in its fine pot, purely for my school kids, of course, not for me personally. Yes, just for my pupils to learn from and you all can take all the rest to share between you - if that's all agreeable to you agreeable folks."

Fred was stunned, "What?"

Pegg smiled quietly, "I'll take the aspidistra. All right Uncle Fred?"

Fred stood up shakily and raised his hand like a traffic policeman, "Over my dead body."

Old Pegg surveyed Uncle Fred, looking him up and down, "That shouldn't take too long to arrange, judging by the look of you. Why, you're falling apart. Do you eat?"

Fred looked miserable, "Not much." He conceded as the others edged away from him.

Pegg continued sarcastically, "Well, why not give it up completely and then your condition for giving me the aspidistra can be met."

Fred's jaw dropped and he asked numbly, "What condition?"

"Over your dead body, of course." Pegg looked at the coffin apologetically, "I beg your pardon Aunt Agatha. No offense Ma'am to you. Only a figure of speech - just a general term of abuse to let Fred know what I think of him."

Fred, the undertaker, appeared to be on the point of tears, "Oh I was so happy as a gravedigger in the good old days before the war. I need that aspidistra for my chapel."

The gypsy, Officer Charlie and Kate all began to make their claims.

"And I want it for my consulting room."

"And I want it for my front porch where I train young policemen to serve the needy community."

"And I just want it - because its purty."

At this point, there was a knock on the door. Kate suddenly and tearfully opened it without asking who was there, or even referring to Officer Charlie.

A tall gentleman entered. He was of a professional appearance. He was dressed in a formal dark suit and overcoat and hat, black shoes and carried a briefcase. He nodded to the others, looked at Auntie Agatha, sighed and placed his briefcase on the table and took out the will. He then sat down. He reminded the mourners that he was their nephew Twoomey, the lawyer. He waved casually at Aunt

Agatha and sighed, "Ah, she looks so well. Isn't she so like herself."

Fred, the undertaker, who took all the credit for Aunt Agatha's appearance thanked Twoomey in real humility.

Kate was still tearful, "Oh yes, her dying suddenly, like that, did her appearance the world of good."

Twoomey was a little taken aback, "Amen. Oh yes, of course. Thank you my dear relatives for gathering together here tonight. I have here the last will and testament of our dear departed Auntie Agatha. I will read it just as she wrote it with her winsome aphorisms."

Kate and Gypsy looked at each other with raised eyebrows. They shrugged blankly as the lawyer primly cleared his throat once or twice. "I'm afraid there was little to bequeath. The kitchen equipment to Sister Kate for her new house - wherever she may be able to get one. The soft furnishings to Cousin Gypsy for her future marriage, if anyone will have her at her age. The furniture to Charlie for his front porch - it's all it's good for. The paintings and decorations to Uncle Fred for his chapel of rest. The books and writing materials to Granny Pegg for her pupils who so badly need some sort of real help in learning." He looked around with finality. "This ends the bequests. Auntie Agatha left no money. Any questions?"

Several of the mourners asked at the same time, "Yes, who gets the aspidistra? You didn't say."

The lawyer replied, "Of course not, I haven't come to the terms and conditions. I have just read the bequests. The aspidistra was not bequeathed. It was included in the terms of her interment - to be buried with her in her grave. The pot between her hands for all eternity, the plant to grow out of her last resting place. Obviously a shallow grave is called for. As executor I intend to carry out all the terms of her last wishes."

Pegg, Charlie, Kate and Gypsy began to mutter underneath their breath. Their comments were not very complimentary to the lawyer.

"I'll bet you do."

"Oh really - you squirt."

"How could you subject that poor plant to such a fate."

"You're going to bury the pot of gold, too?"

Twoomey shuffled together his papers and placed them carefully back into his briefcase, "Those are the terms - exactly. I intend to ensure that they are followed to the letter."

Fred, the old undertaker, rolled his eyes in horror staring at the ceiling, "There is no deed of man so foul, so vile that cannot be made to look normal and harmless by comparison with even worse, even more horrendous acts of abomination and hatred, perpetrated by other men in other times and places."

Fred turned to Cousin Twoomey, "Yes other men like you, Twoomey. You poking, prying, lied up, dried up, slick old pickpocket – you'll see us all cheated. How do we know that will is genuine?"

The lawyer stood up and straightened his shoulders briskly, "That's quite enough, ladies and gentlemen. As executor, I'll have the plant and pot removed and buried with Auntie Agatha at a secret time of the funeral. I will also have the exact location disguised, i.e., a secret reburial to protect from graverobbers. And I'll see to it that the will is admitted to probate forthwith. If any of you wish to dispute any term of the will, I suggest you see a lawyer. Good day."

The lawyer packed his briefcase and left, bowed at the door and closed it gently behind him.

Officer Charlie shook his head sadly, "Well, that's it. To think that he too is one of our family."

Kate was still stunned, "So the best part is to be buried with the old lady."

Pegg wiped away a tear, "Auntie Agatha put her whole life's savings into that golden pot and plant. She cheated us all. How she must be laughing at us."

Even the gypsy admitted, "I could never have foretold this disaster."

Fred once again began to reminisce in his usual nostalgic way, "Oh dear, there are no rewards for education and ambition nowadays, the way there used to be in the good old days before the war. Oh how I wish that once again I was a happy gravedigger."

They all left slowly, bowed over and miserable. Just then the daylight began to fade as the sun went down behind the trees.

END OF STORY

The Playscript

PRODUCTION NOTES
Stage Time: About 70-100 minutes.
One Set - One Scene
Setting Time: The near Past or Present
Actors: Three males, three females, one deceased (prop or person).
Music: Three songs: *Fish and Chips, Dream Back the Good Dreams, Gold Bugs.*

OUTLINE OF THE PLAY
ACT ONE - THE LAST SIGHTS
Scene One - Secretary and the Undertaker
Scene Two - The Cop and the Gypsy
ACT TWO - WHO GETS WHAT?
Scene One - The Schoolmarm and the Mouthpiece
Scene Two - Life Goes On

THE MAIN CHARACTERS
UNCLE FRED:
The undertaker and an elderly relative of the deceased.
AUNTIE AGATHA:
The dear departed, laid out on view in her coffin.
GYPSY POSEY:
A niece and a fortuneteller by profession.
SISTER KATE:
Younger sister of the deceased, hostess of the viewing.

COUSIN CHARLIE:
A policeman and a relative.
GRANMA PEGGY:
A schoolteacher, related to Aunt Agatha.
NEPHEW TWOOMEY:
A lawyer, also related

****

ACT ONE - THE LAST SIGHTS
SCENE ONE
THE SECRETARY AND THE UNDERTAKER

This is a short comedy about the last viewing, by friends, of an old lady, now deceased. The scene is set in the parlor of the dear departed Auntie Agatha.

Agatha (actor or prop) lies in her coffin, center-stage, tilted slightly towards the audience, for a last viewing by her relatives. She wears a white shroud, her hands are folded across her chest. She is white haired and elderly. Left-stage, also slanted towards the audience is a large aspidistra in a gold and silver pot and the rest of the room is lined with regular living room furniture - such as dining table, chairs, sofas, rocking chair, cabinet, piano, desk-bureau and fireplace with mantle. There are some sandwiches and drinks on the table, in expectation of visitors.

Downstage, across the backdrop area and stage right and left are the walls of the parlor or living room with old fashioned pictures. Near center on backdrop there is an outer door. The floor should have rugs and either lino or carpet. Near center along one wall is a full length closet or cupboard, closed at present. Behind the door of the cupboard or closet are lined up garden implements, spades, shovels, rakes and hoes.

Along the left wall of the parlor is an open doorway leading to the kitchen. In all, a comfortable parlor with oldish furniture that contrasts with the large flashy aspidistra in the gold and silver pot along the left wall - a scene that could be set almost anywhere in the world.

Sister Kate, mid-aged, in white blouse, piled-up hair, long black skirt, is crossing the stage, opens door and admits Uncle Fred.

Enter Uncle Fred the Undertaker, *an elderly man dressed in old fashioned gentlemanly style in hat, gloves, dark formal clothes, and black shoes, white shirt, black tie. Fred is shaky and trembling in voice and gesture, with age and infirmity. All of Uncle Fred's misquotations from great poets are, of course, phony (though perhaps reminiscent). He enters, still holding the door open, hands on chest, with gravity.*

He approaches the coffin, rubs his hands together as one satisfied with his handiwork in setting up the display containing Auntie Agatha. He then looks around.

Sings: **FISH AND CHIPS**

Sung: Fast

VERSE 1 AND REFRAIN:

s d - d m s d^1 t
O I'll have some fish and chips please
d^1 r^1 l - l - l - l
If that's all right with you
f r - r - r f t - t - t
Not too much grease - some mushy peas
l s s s - f m
And salt and vinegar too
s d - d m - s d^1 - d^1 t
No more the dainty dinner do
d^1 r^1 l - l - l - l
No more them dunking dips
l s s - s s - t t l
I say if it's all right with you
s - s s f r d
I'll have some fish and chips

VERSE 1 AND REFRAIN:

O I'll have some fish and chips please
If that's all right with you
Not too much grease - some mushy peas
And salt and vinegar too
No more the dainty dinner do
No more them dunking dips
I say if it's all right with you
I'll have some fish and chips.

VERSE 2:
Now the Admiral was in the pink
His ships were spiffy clean
Your Majesty what do you think?
He asks the blooming Queen
Says the Queen I absolutely love
This fleet of men and ships
The only thing they need more of
Is good old fish and chips.

VERSE 3:
Well my Uncle Ray drops dead one day
We lay him down in flowers
Then we start a party right away
To brighten those sad hours
Ahh . . . suddenly he bolts upright
And fear and terror grips . . .
We ask - What brought you back? He cried
I smell some fish and chips.

VERSE 4:
See I knew a glamour girl I say
As pretty as the moon
Says she - Come visit me some day -
So I showed up right soon
She asked - What would you like to do?
And smiled those lovely lips
I said - If it's all right with you
We'll have some fish and chips.

SISTER KATE: This is a wake – not a fish and chip shop.

UNCLE FRED: *(subdued)* Ah, Sister Kate. How do you like my handiwork? I sent her here earlier you know. *(looks around disappointed at furniture but brightens when he sees aspidistra)*

SISTER KATE: I know, Uncle Fred. You did a good job in setting her up. *(looks at the coffin sadly)* She's very like herself, so she is.

UNCLE FRED: *(keenly)* Aye - Very lifelike, that's true. I've never seen her look better. She glows with brightness and beauty. *(sighs, holding his chin)* Aye, that last illness of hers must have done her a world of good.

SISTER KATE: *(querulously)* But she's dead. Isn't she?

UNCLE FRED: Of course, but I mean a world of good in her appearance, although we morticians add a little makeup too - so maybe I should take the credit. But sometimes illness makes one look better *(taps his midriff)* reduces weight perhaps.

SISTER KATE: *(looks at her midriff)* Oh yes, I wish I could take sick at times. It must be very good for one's health.

UNCLE FRED: *(formally)* The dear departed being my favorite aunt, I am, of course, offering the funeral services, including dressing and display that you see here *(he points to the coffin)* - entirely free of charge - a small service to our family . . .

SISTER KATE: *(miserably)* We're all very grateful. *(weeps slightly)*

UNCLE FRED: Poor Auntie Agatha would not have left anywhere near as much as it would have taken to employ our services. These few sticks of furniture - pathetic. Ah, it is so sad to see that after a lifetime of hard and faithful work, the poor departed leaves only a few sticks - none of which I am personally interested in, I may say.

Sister Kate subtly positions herself between Fred and the aspidistra. She is slightly protective. Noticing this, Fred looks around her at the aspidistra.

UNCLE FRED: Of course, my only aim is for the good of the community as a whole. Perhaps some small thing of no value to enhance the funeral chapel and to enrich the lives of the bereaved widows and orphans who go there to weep and mourn their dear departed. Ah, yes, some little brightening token to cheer them up. Perhaps I might be constrained upon to accept some such *(looking enviously at the aspidistra)* small toy, some bauble, valueless in itself but bringing joy to the heart of the poor, the stricken, the mournful.

SISTER KATE: *(eagerly)* You mean like balloons. Yes. . . I'm sure . . .

UNCLE FRED: *(outraged)* What do you mean, Sister Kate, by "balloons"! Balloons, Ma'am. *(thundering)* What of balloons?

SISTER KATE: *(innocently)* Little red and blue and green plastic bags of air to cheer up the orphans.

UNCLE FRED: How dare you, Ma'am! How dare you insult those poor little orphans. Whoever heard of balloons at a funeral service? Why do you think the bereaved attend - to celebrate? Who, who Ma'am would want to celebrate the passing of a relative? . . Who? Who? Answer me, who?

SISTER KATE: *(evasively)* Well, it would depend on the relative, wouldn't it Uncle Fred? What about the piano? I'm sure no one would object to your taking the old - I mean the genuine antique - piano?

UNCLE FRED: *(sighing)* No, we already have two pianos. No, I wouldn't want anything as valuable as that - just that silly aspidistra would cheer up the orphans and widows so well . . .

SISTER KATE: *(stamping her foot)* Over my dead body! *(to Auntie Agatha)* Oh, I beg your pardon Auntie - no offence intended. *(to Fred)* You can't have it. O.K?

UNCLE FRED: *(eagerly)* And why not? What if Auntie Agatha wanted me to have it? The will has not been read, has it? You didn't see the will did you?

SISTER KATE: No, I didn't. But I know for a fact that Auntie Agatha did not want you to have it. I was her secretary - voluntary, of course - for her last years.

UNCLE FRED: Hmm, ah, now I see. She didn't like me, did she? So why am I burying her free, eh? I wonder?

SISTER KATE: *(evasively)* Who said she didn't like you? She liked you a lot. I only said . . .

UNCLE FRED: I know what you said but I also know what Auntie Agatha thought about me.

SISTER KATE: How could you?

UNCLE FRED: Because secretaries are like dogs.

SISTER KATE: What?

UNCLE FRED: Yes, dogs always give their owners away. The dog barks and snarls when you approach – it's only acting out the sneers and groans and stiffness it picks up from its owner when he sees you coming. It doesn't have the sophistication to fake a liking for you. Yes, secretaries are the same. The subtle clues of dislike, disdain, distrust of me that you picked up from Auntie Agatha - all came out in your big ugly clock when I used to visit you and Auntie Agatha - your clock certainly tells the time – I'll say that for you.

SISTER KATE: *(smiling weakly)* It's not true. I'm just downcast at dear Auntie's death.

UNCLE FRED: Don't fool me. You were always frowning and tense every time I ever visited dear old Auntie Agatha. *(he reconsiders)* Well . . anyhow, if the rest of the family agree that I should have a small reward, it's very likely that you'll agree too. *(holding his lapel and shaking his head sadly)* After all, it's only to brighten things up for the widows and orphans in my chapel of remembrance.

SISTER KATE: Why not charge them a little less, then they'll be really grateful?

UNCLE FRED: Oh dear, this is too much for me. I wish I was a poor gravedigger again, like in the good old days before the war.

Fred draws himself up to his full height with dignity, opens his mouth as if to say something more, is lost for words, shakes his head in disgust and proceeds to examine the gold pot holding the aspidistra.

UNCLE FRED: *(pleased)* Yes, very nice, solid gold with inlaid silver - very nice indeed . . . Just right for the First Chapel of Rest.

Kate folds her arms and stamps her foot in disdain.

SISTER KATE: Why are chapels and churches always being set against each other, like racing greyhounds, first, second, third Baptist or Presbyterian. There must be better or more spiritual ways to distinguish one church from another. It's so childish. It's like kids saying *(she sticks her tongue out and puts her fingers in her ears)*

Ya, ya, ya. Boo, boo, boo. Boo, boo, boo
Boo, boo, boo. Hiss, hiss, hiss. Ya, ya, ya
We were here first. We were here first. We were here first. Why not, not you? How did you miss? Ha, ha, ha.

UNCLE FRED: *(smugly)* Well, it's nice to be a winner, like First Chapel of Rest.

SISTER KATE: Oh, yes, you hardly ever hear of a fourth or fifth church or a 22nd one. Only the three top medal winners, but especially number one. *(she cocks her head quizzically at Fred)*

Fred places hand on hip and glares back at Kate. They stick out their fingers in their ears and tongues at each other.

Curtain

ACT ONE - THE LAST SIGHTS

SCENE TWO

THE COP AND THE GYPSY

The same, all is as before. Sister Kate and Uncle Fred are still on stage, still making negative gestures at each other. Kate is shaking fists, Fred is wagging index finger, both are puffing and blowing and then turn their back on each other, as there is a knock on the door. Fred turns again to examine the aspidistra and Kate opens the door.

***Enter Cousin Charlie**, dressed as a law officer, who salutes all and sundry, in a somewhat vacant manner. Sings – **FISH AND CHIPS**.*

FISH AND CHIPS

VERSE 3:
Well my Uncle Ray drops dead one day
We lay him down in flowers
Then we start a party right away
To brighten those sad hours
Ahh . . . suddenly he bolts upright
And fear and terror grips . . .
We ask - What brought you back? He cried
I smell some fish and chips.

VERSE 4:
See I knew a glamour girl I say
As pretty as the moon
Says she - Come visit me some day -
So I showed up right soon
She asked - What would you like to do?
And smiled those lovely lips
I said - If it's all right with you
We'll have some fish and chips.

COUSIN CHARLIE: *(to Kate)* Now Sister Kate, I've warned you many times - not to open the door like that without finding out who is outside.

KATE: *(naively)* But if I hadn't opened the door Charlie, how could you have come in?

CHARLIE: *(with just a little severity)* But how did you know it was me?

KATE: Well, I was right, wasn't I?

CHARLIE: *(slowly, syllable by syllable)* Look, everybody who was ever murdered by an intruder had been right in opening doors and letting people in - on every occasion in their life except the last one. See? *(reverting to normal speech)* Now, tell me, why did you open the door - just like that?

KATE: *(self righteously)* Charlie, it was you who knocked the door. Now . . you know you did. Isn't that true? *(to Fred)* Charlie knocked, didn't he?

Fred nods vacantly, still examining the pot of gold.

CHARLIE: *(somewhat outraged, shaking his head in officious disdain)* Doors are meant to keep people out not to let people in. If we just wanted to let people in we could live outdoors and provide a lawn for our visitors. Heck no. Doors are meant to keep out humans and dogs. See . . an open door is a contradiction in terms, a paradox, an oxymoron and a very dangerous incongruity. Ahem . . a car that does not drive, a plane that doesn't fly is all the same as a door that does not stay closed. Hmm . . see? Anyone who opens a door just because someone knocks it, doesn't need a door, doesn't deserve a door. Why not just leave a hole in the wall? Or live in a cave?

KATE: But, Cousin Charlie, that way it would get cold in here. And besides, anyone could just walk in through a hole in the wall. So don't be silly.

CHARLIE: *(dazed by Kate's logic)* Well, that's exactly what I mean, anyone could just walk in if you open the door just because someone knocks.

KATE: Oh no they couldn't, Charlie.

CHARLIE: And why not?

KATE: Because I closed it immediately after you came in. And besides, you wouldn't let them, would you Charlie?

CHARLIE: *(still dazed)* Who me?

KATE: Yes, you wouldn't let them.

CHARLIE: Let them what?

KATE: Let just anyone walk in, would you?

CHARLIE: *(uncertainly)* Well . . no . . .

KATE: See! You're a policeman, aren't you?

CHARLIE: *(confused but proud)* Oh, yes. Yes, of course. *(straightening his shoulders)* Sure, sure, I'm a policeman. I just want you to be safe.

KATE: Well then, what have I got to worry about?

CHARLIE: *(still confused)* O, I see. You mean you're safe on <u>this</u> occasion?

KATE: *(smiling)* Exactly, Charlie. That's what I've been trying to say to you.

Charlie passes his open palms across his eyes - shakes his head to clear his thinking and then walks over reverently to view Auntie Agatha.

CHARLIE: Ah, what a fine figure of a gentlewoman, my own dear departed Aunt Agatha. *(looks more closely at Aunt Agatha)* Hmm, who trussed her up like this? I suppose it was you, Fred? Is this kidnapping, I wonder? *(he scratches his head, quizzically)*

FRED: Kidnapping? What do you mean? The deceased has to be strapped in, in case she falls out.

CHARLIE: How could she? She's dead, isn't she?

FRED: *(seriously)* Oh, she's dead all right. But what if someone slipped while carrying the coffin?

CHARLIE: *(sarcastically)* Oh, I see. I thought perhaps you were afraid she might escape.

FRED: *(shaking his head seriously)* Oh no. There's no chance of that.

Sings: **DREAM BACK THE GOOD DREAMS**
Sung: Medium Slow and Nostalgic

VERSE 1:
d m m m m r d m - s
We'll dream of the good dreams gone by
l *s*
And sigh
l s m d - d r m l_1
We'll dream of our dreams way back then
d m m m m
When all of our days
r d m - s l - s
We were dreaming always
l s m d r m r *d*
We'll dream back the good dreams again

REFRAIN:
m s s s s l t - d^1
We'll sing of the good songs gone by
l - d^1
And cry
l s m d d r m l_1
We'll sing all the songs we sang then
d m m m m
For all the day long
r d m - s l - s
We were singing a song
l s m d r m r *d*
We'll sing back the good songs again

VERSE 1:
We'll dream of the good dreams gone by
And sigh
We'll dream of our dreams way back then
When all of our days
We were dreaming always
We'll dream back the good dreams again.

VERSE 2:
We'll sing of the good songs gone by
And cry
We'll sing all the songs we sang then
For all the day long
We were singing a song
We'll sing back the good songs again.

VERSE 3:
The dancers of night will dance by
And fly
Too quickly old dancing does end
But we'll dance until dawn
And the night fear is gone
And we'll dance the old dancing again.

CHARLIE: *(shaking his head)* I know. I know. Only kidding, Fred. Why are people so humorless on these occasions? Once you fellows get your hands on a body, it's all up, isn't it? I mean, all down, you know - ha, ha. No jail breaks from you lot eh? So everyone sits around with faces as long as a gravedigger's shovel. Come on, cheer up.

FRED: *(plaintively)* Oh dear. I wish I was a poor gravedigger again, just like in the good old days before the war. This is much too much for me.

Fred looks pained but smiles slightly. Charlie begins to notice and take an interest in the gold-potted aspidistra. He looks it over. There is another knock on the door.

CHARLIE: *(to Sister Kate)* Ah, ah, ah - remember?

FRED: *(to Charlie)* You're paranoid.

CHARLIE: You'd be insane not to be paranoid in this life.

KATE: *(opening door)* Who's there?

VOICE: Your niece, Gypsy Posey.

Enter Gypsy Posey, *a fortuneteller in colorful formal dress with long black hair tied* *back, and deep dark eyes. Sings –* ***FISH AND CHIPS****.*

VERSE 4:
See I knew a handsome man I say
As cheerful as the moon
Says he - Come visit me some day -
So I showed up right soon
He asked - What would you like to do?
We've some nice river trips
I said - If it's all right with you
We'll have some fish and chips

GYPSY: Good luck to all here. May everyone here enjoy long life and happiness. *(she approaches and looks at Auntie Agatha and hesitates)* Oh, I beg your pardon, Auntie Agatha. No offence intended. *(dabs her eyes)* Oh, it was so unexpected and sudden.

FRED: Well, of course, she was 99 and suffered from a bad heart - so it shouldn't have been all that unexpected. Ah, if only people would look ahead a little and plot their plots.

GYPSY: *(brightening)* Pay you up front, you mean. Yes, that's what I tell them. Look ahead

- through the tea leaves. It's worth the small fee I charge.

FRED: *(mournfully)* Well, we all should know that we can't last forever. A little financial planning for the planting and her funeral could have been paid for in advance - as it is, I am donating all the funeral services, including the dressing of the corpse as you see. *(he points to Auntie Agatha and then links his hands together primly in front of his chest)* And all I am asking in return, dear niece Gypsy, if you all approve, is this little old aspidistra to grace my chapel.

Gypsy looks with interest at the plant.

CHARLIE: *(still examining the gold pot)* Who assayed this gold?

GYPSY: *(with astonishment)* Gold? Real gold? Oh, dear Aunt Aggie had such good taste. She was such a wonderful person.

FRED: Yes, but all good things must pass away. Just like the bad things of life. Alas, where are the ladies of days gone?
Fred bows to the others - A question asked by the great French Poet - Villon.

He mispronounces the word to sound like 'villain.'

CHARLIE: Are you calling me a scoundrel, Uncle Fred?

FRED: *(surprised)* Why no, cousin Charlie. Certainly not.

CHARLIE: Only my boss calls me names - that way I get paid for it. See?

FRED: Of course Charlie, it must be a misunderstanding.

GYPSY: *(looking at the aspidistra)* This would be ideal for my consulting room.

CHARLIE: With the kind of clients you have, that thing would be gone the first time you left the room. It would look much nicer and be a lot safer on my porch.

GYPSY: O, but I never leave my clients alone in the room. What do you take me for? *(positively)* It's a professional office - not a hotel, you know.

CHARLIE: I'm glad to hear it. Just how exactly would you describe your practice? Witchcraft? Voodoo? Séance? Mumbo Jumbo?

GYPSY: No, no. You know perfectly well that I'm merely a fortuneteller.

CHARLIE: Aha, a crystal ball gazer eh? That's what I suspected, that's what I heard. Charging people for telling fortunes with cards, tea leaves or crystals is against the law around here.

GYPSY: Oh, everything is against the law nowadays. There's laws against guns, laws against every known trade and profession and business unless you have a license, laws against using your house for a business, laws against drugs and even alcohol in times and places and every single one of your silly laws is just there to protect vested interests and keep the newcomers from making a living.

CHARLIE: Really? First I heard of it. So who are the insider fortunetellers I'm protecting? Eh?

GYPSY: Oh, you don't know? The religion industry, of course and meteorologists and psychologists and psychiatrists and economists - there are plenty of them and they foretell it all wrong just as often as I do. If I had a Ph.D. in Economics, I could fortune tell to my heart's content, get it wrong every time and still make a pretty penny. All right?

CHARLIE: *(defensively)* Well, at least economists can make an educated guess. You can't!

GYPSY: So I should use math models to base my false predictions on - then I'd still be wrong, dead wrong but on the right side of the law, eh? *(tearfully)* It seems to me that most of your laws are there merely to prevent the have-nots from becoming haves. Nothing against the economist who is lying but all against a poor lady fortuneteller who only tries to make people happy. All your laws do is keep the hungry outsiders out and keep the greedy insiders in. Greed, you know, is the root of all evil according to the good book.

Charlie shrugs and looks mystified.

KATE: I think you're both in the wrong. This aspidistra should go to me as a reward for my secretarial - part-time but voluntary - services to Auntie Agatha for so many months before her beloved departure.

FRED: Well, you all want it for yourselves, your homes *(aside* - What does she mean by beloved departure?*)* But I would agree to resolve this stalemate, this potential family row. Believe me, I am prepared to resolve this dispute, act as a good Samaritan - a peacemaker – not, I say *(eagerly)* by taking this plant for myself but rather by mediating . . .

KATE, CHARLIE, GYPSY: *(in unison)* Yes, how?

FRED: Well, acting purely for the public good *(he smiles hollowly)* and without serving any personal motive - it could be placed in the First Chapel of Rest . . .

CHARLIE: *(in a cold tone - sitting down)* As a public service?

GYPSY: *(with raised eyebrows)* Not to enhance your private business as an undertaker?

KATE: *(sarcastically)* Just to cheer up the orphans?

FRED: *(pleased and unaware of the sarcasm)* Right, exactly.

GYPSY: I know something else you could do for the orphans.

FRED: Yes, dear niece, what is that?

GYPSY: *(coldly)* Stop ripping them off, so that they wouldn't have to spend half their lives saving up just to end up dead and dumped in your rubbish heap for dead bodies. Your human garbage pile with flowers on top.

All three glare, unfriendily, at Uncle Fred who looks miserable.

FRED: *(miserably)* Oh, I used to be so happy as a young and carefree and innocent gravedigger, in the good old days before the war. The war ruined everything. People just aren't the same. Boo. Hoo. Hoo. *(he weeps)* I remember the time when *(pointing accusingly at Charlie)* people didn't even bother to lock their doors never mind worry about opening them. Before you cops got your computers, cars, spy systems and started taping everyone. For all your spying and taping, crime has gone through the roof.

CHARLIE: *(shrugging)* What am I supposed to do about it?

FRED: Do what you all did before - when crime was low. . .

CHARLIE: What's that?

FRED: Simple: Get back on the street, on the beat, on your feet.

Charlie is stunned, raises his feet and looks at them, dumbfounded, stands up suddenly and salutes the audience.
All sing: ***WE'LL DREAM BACK***

Curtain

ACT TWO - WHO GETS WHAT?

SCENE ONE

THE SCHOOLMARM AND THE MOUTHPIECE

The same, all is as before except that all four characters are now standing looking at the aspidistra set in its golden pot. The challenge: Let's compromise and share.

GYPSY: Look, it's so silly arguing about who gets the aspidistra. When the will is read, nephew Twoomey, the executor will make sure it goes to the one that Auntie Agatha willed it to. Now the only way around that is if we can all agree.

CHARLIE: That's right, we can all agree on what to do with our own property.

UNCLE FRED: So let's agree on something . . but what?

KATE: Well, the aspidistra with its gold pot is very valuable. There's no doubt about that. Why Auntie Agatha just almost worshipped it - she said it was the culmination of her life's work - she wouldn't even let me water it - she doted on it. So, since it's worth a lot, why don't we agree to sell it and share out the profits - no matter who gets it. Now, if Granma Pegg - she should be along soon - agrees, we'll split it five ways – isn't that fair?

FRED: *(reluctantly)* I suppose so.

GYPSY: *(keenly)* Of course . . it's fair. That gold pot is an antique. It could be worth a fortune. Now 20% of 100,000 is 20,000 – that's better than a poke in the eye with a sharp stick.

CHARLIE: *(thoughtfully)* Yes, let's all agree . . .

GYPSY: Right. Let's all shake on it and when Gran Pegg comes let's all act real casual and not act like it's worth a whole lot so that she'll agree. After all, if one person contested us on behalf of the will, it could cost us a pretty penny in legal fees.

They all shake hands and smile and agree. Pleased with the deal, Uncle Fred poses beside the coffin, places one hand on the coffin and the other on his lapel. The others stand by and listen politely, smiling cheerfully and nodding to each other in appreciation of his offering.

FRED: Yes, let's look on the bright side - every cloud has a silver lining.

KATE: Oh, what a wonderful original thought!

UNCLE FRED: *(speaking loudly and poetically)* Alas we pass like flotsam on the shores of life. *(all agree tearfully)*

He points, still standing in door, to imaginary driftwood.

Longfeller, my dear Sister Kate, ah . . .
Longfeller *(he bows low)*

SISTER KATE: O do invite him in, Fred, all mourners *(she sniffs and dabs her nose)* are welcome - no matter how tall.

UNCLE FRED: *(looks out, mystified)* There's no one there.

SISTER KATE: *(dimly and shakily)* I thought you said there was a skinny chap outside.

UNCLE FRED: Dear me, no. *(closes door, confused)* No, no. A misunderstanding, my dear Sister Kate. I thought I was quoting Longfellow but perhaps it was the great Irish Poet - Yeats.

KATE: What?

FRED: *(to Kate)* Yeats, Ma'am, Yeats.

He pronounces it to rhyme with eats.

KATE: *(lifting a small tray of goodies and passing it to Uncle Fred and others while smiling sweetly)* Oh yes, we've plenty of eats - have a salad sandwich.

FRED: No thanks. You must have misunderstood. No, I'm trying to lose weight. Food is bad for you. Auntie Agatha ate and ate all her life and *(shaking his head sadly)* just look what it did to her at the end.

GYPSY: *(motioning to the coffin)* But everyone ends up like this.

FRED: *(fearfully)* Exactly and everyone eats, don't they? Eating is a much overrated pastime, Ma'am. *(shakes his head)* It overtaxes the system, yes Ma'am.

The others eat and drink a little, still nodding politely to each other. There is a knock on the door. Kate approaches the door sedately, smiling at Cousin Charlie, who nods approvingly.

KATE: *(still looking at Charlie)* Who's there?

VOICE: Granny Pegg.

CHARLIE: *(to Kate)* Hold on. Just a minute. *(to others)* Look Granny Pegg is a tough old schoolmarm. *(he waves his hand negatively)* Once she makes up her mind about anything - she'll never change it. Let's make sure we do a good job of *(lowers his voice)* persuading her on what we're all agreed upon.

OTHERS: *(nodding in agreement)* Sure. Yes. Alright.

CHARLIE: *(continuing)* So let's all sit down and look real casual and pay no special attention to that aspidistra. It's of no account - get it?

Others agree and sit down with their drinks or sandwiches, posing casually and politely.

CHARLIE: *(continuing)* I'll give her some soft soap about the teaching profession. Then we can casually mention that we've agreed to share everything equally. Get it?

Charlie nods to Kate, who opens the door and admits Granny Pegg.

Enter Granny Pegg, *severely dressed in tweed costume, high flat walking shoes, large old fashioned hat and scarf. She is quite elderly. She nods to the family members who nod back, dabbing their eyes and sniffing.*

GRANNY PEGG: Good afternoon, Charlie, Fred, Gypsy and dear Kate.

Kate embraces her tearfully and kisses her.

KATE: Dear Granny.

The others, while sniffing occasionally, make deliberate attempts to be casual. Crossing legs. Looking at ceiling. Much shaking heads, sighing and polishing of fingernails on clothes.

Granny Pegg is a stern and aggressive, old lady. All her actions and words make it clear that she is decisive, no nonsense, loud and sure of herself. She approaches the coffin and looks at Auntie Agatha.

CHARLIE: I appreciate what you're doing Granny Pegg, trying to blow away cobwebs of ignorance, smarten up young people and straighten out their ideas on goodness and helping their neighbor. The golden rule and all that, yessir Gran. Greed is bad enough but dumbness and ignorance make this poor life even more of a misery. A good schoolteacher does a real good job.

KATE: Oh, I just loved all my schoolteachers. They were so kind to me, I never learned hardly anything at all - I was so happy.

CHARLIE: I can believe that. But, see, it's like this, a savvy stockbroker or a smart-aleck lawyer doesn't need to rip you off. He can make heap plenty green stuff just doing his regular thing. Dumb money advisors and numbskull attorneys, dunce real estate agents and the like are too stupid and incompetent to make money except by cheating you. Same with honest, I mean honest-to-goodness thieves - a smart housebreaker cum burglar will make sure, by checking around, whether there is someone at home. A dumb thief will knock on the front door only, get no reply and just bust in. Then lo and behold, the owner is there at the back, sleeping or deaf or just not answering the door and next thing you know there's a confrontation and the house owner maybe gets killed.

KATE: But Charlie, you said not to answer the door just a little while ago. You said . . . *(to Fred)* Didn't he Fred?

FRED: *(to Charlie)* Yes you did . . . You said, Never answer the door. We all heard you distinctly. Didn't we?

The others nod.

CHARLIE: *(stiffly)* Not at all - I said nothing of the kind - always answer, speak to the door, some thief could be testing to see if there's anyone at home. See? What I said was - do not open the door. Anyhow, Granny Pegg, I appreciate you spreading knowledge, helping kids to wise-up, teaching morals is all great work. Dumbness plus ignorance is a bad combination. Yes, Granny Pegg, teaching is one necessary and one honorable profession. I'm sure I speak for the whole family and the entire neighborhood when I say . . .

PEGG: *(distressed)* How could anyone die who looks so well? What a fine head of hair. Are you sure that she got proper medical treatment?

KATE: Oh, yes Granny. In fact she had a specialist.

PEGG: *(suspiciously)* What kind of specialist?

KATE: Well, you got me there. *(looking at others)* What kind of specialist? *(the others shake their heads)* But I do know that she had a specialist. *(brightening)* Oh, I think he was a heart specialist - yes, a cardiologist. *(smiling)* Yes, a cardio - or was it a gerontologist - Oh, well, it was some kind of an 'ologist' anyway.

PEGG: Some folks know when they're about to go and some folks don't. The one sort lives about as long as the other. A specialist only tells you the bad news - he doesn't know enough to save you from it. Ah, yes. All they know is their own specialty - did anyone ever visit a specialist who didn't need that specialist?

The others look blank and shrug.

I'm asking a serious question. Did anyone not need one who ever visited one? Did anyone ever visit any eye specialist and the eye specialist tell them - Oh, you don't need an eye specialist, you need a nerve or a psychology or a back pain specialist? Since I can't help there will be no fee. What rubbish! Specialists all believe they can cure anything – they're quacks.

No wonder poor Aunt Agatha succumbed to neglect and misunderstanding and physicians. Tragic. Poor lady. Bah! Specialists. I'm asking a serious question since I'm now entering the second half of my life when advancing years take their toll.

Gypsy looks puzzled and counts her fingers, raises her eyebrows to the audience.

GYPSY: *(aside)* What's she mean - now entering the second half of her life? How long does she think she's going to live? To be a hundred and sixty? *(points a finger at Granny Pegg)*

PEGG: Bah, doctors. A doctor is the last person you need *(nodding significantly)* the very last.

KATE: No. That's a cruel thing to say.

PEGG: No? Well, very well, I take that back - AN UNDERTAKER is the very last person you need. A doctor is the second . . ah, the next to last person you need.

KATE: Now Granny Pegg. You're saying that specialist doctors are money grabbers who'll sell you any old trashy treatment. The doctors that I know are there to help whether they make money or not.

PEGG: Altruism - philanthropy - do goodism whatever you want to call it, is like the ghost and the vampire and the English Constitution. Libraries of books, professors, degrees, schools, whole industries have flourished on it but when you want to see it, it can't be found. Seems like it doesn't even exist. Taint there.

(looking at aspidistra) But this does exist and is very, very interesting. Hmm. That would be nice for my schoolroom - to educate the children on tropical plants, hmm. I wonder to whom Aunt Agatha left this fine specimen?

CHARLIE: *(casually)* Well, Granny, it doesn't matter.

PEGG: Of course it does. What do you mean?

GYPSY: *(eagerly)* Charlie means that since there is no great value in anything and since Auntie Agatha was known to be an eccentric old dear, we're agreed not to go by the literal terms of the will and . . well . . *(suddenly and sharply)* to share everything equally.

FRED: Yes, sell it all and divide the proceeds equally - if that's all right with you. You see there's no one thing of any particular value.

PEGG: *(sharply)* Oh good, good. I'm glad to hear that.

KATE: *(relieved)* So you agree Pegg.

PEGG: Don't be ridiculous. Of course I don't agree. When have I ever agreed to anything in my entire life? When? Tell me, when? *(glares at others)*

GYPSY: *(despondently)* No, you're not known for agreeableness - but we are all agreed.

PEGG: Well that is nice for you. But I am glad to hear, as I said, that there's nothing of any particular value - for I intend to take the plant in its fine pot, purely for my school kids, of course, not for me personally. Yes, just for my pupils to learn from and you all can take all the rest to share between you - if that's all agreeable to you agreeable folks.

FRED: *(stunned)* What?

PEGG: I'll take the aspidistra. All right Uncle Fred?

FRED: *(shakily and standing up)* Over my dead body.

PEGG: That shouldn't take too long to arrange, judging by the look of you - Why, you're falling apart. Do you eat?

FRED: Not much.

PEGG: *(sarcastically)* Well, why not give it up completely and then your condition for giving me the aspidistra can be met.

FRED: *(numbly)* What condition?

PEGG: Over your dead body, of course. *(to coffin)* Beg pardon Aunt Agatha. No offense Ma'am to you. Only a figure of speech - just a general term of abuse to let Fred know what I think of him.

FRED: Oh I was so happy as a gravedigger in the good old days before the war. I need that aspidistra for my chapel.

GYPSY: And I want it for my consulting room.

CHARLIE: And I want it for my front porch where I train young policemen to serve the needy community.

KATE: *(in tears)* And I just want it - because it's purty.

There is a knock on the door. Kate suddenly and tearfully opens it without asking who is there, or even referring to Charlie.

Enter the Lawyer Nephew Twoomey, *dressed in formal dark suit and overcoat and hat, black shoes, carrying a briefcase. He nods to the others, looks at Auntie Agatha, sighs and places his briefcase on the table and takes out the will. Sits down.*

TWOOMEY: Ah, she looks so well. *(smiling)* Isn't she so like herself.

FRED: *(humbly)* Thank you, sir.

KATE: Oh yes, her dying suddenly, like that, did her appearance the world of good.

TWOOMEY: *(taken aback)* Amen. Oh yes, of course. Thank you my dear relatives for gathering together here tonight. I have here the last will and testament of our dear departed Auntie Agatha. I will read it just as she wrote it with her winsome aphorisms.

Kate and Gypsy look at each other with raised eyebrows. They shrug blankly. The lawyer primly clears his throat once or twice.

I'm afraid there was little to bequeath. The kitchen equipment to Sister Kate for her new house - wherever she may be able to get one. The soft furnishings to Cousin Gypsy for her future marriage, if anyone will have her at her age. The furniture to Charlie for his front porch – it's all it's good for. The paintings and decorations to Uncle Fred for his chapel of rest. The books and writing materials to Granny Pegg for her pupils who so badly need some sort of real help in learning. *(looks around)* This ends the bequests. Auntie Agatha left no money. Any questions?

CHARLIE: Yes, who gets the aspidistra? You didn't say.

TWOOMEY: Of course not. I haven't come to the terms and conditions. I have just read the bequests. The aspidistra was not bequeathed. It was included in the terms of her interment - to be buried with her in her grave. The pot between her hands for all eternity, the plant to grow out of her last resting place. Obviously a shallow grave is called for. As executor I intend to carry out all the terms of her last wishes.

PEGG: *(to Twoomey)* I'll bet you do.

CHARLIE: *(to Twoomey)* Oh really - you squirt.

KATE: *(to Twoomey)* How could you subject that poor plant to such a fate.

GYPSY: *(to Twoomey)* You're going to bury the pot of gold, too?

TWOOMEY: Exactly - those are the terms. I intend to ensure that they are followed to the letter.

FRED: *(in horror, staring at the ceiling)* There is no deed of man so foul, so vile that cannot be made to look normal and harmless by comparison with even worse, even more horrendous acts of abomination and hatred, perpetrated by other men in other times and places.

(turning to Cousin Twoomey) Yes other men like you, Twoomey. You poking, prying, lied up, dried up, slick old pickpocket - you'll see us all cheated. How do we know that will is genuine?

TWOOMEY: *(standing up)* That's quite enough, ladies and gentlemen. As executor, I'll have the plant and pot removed and buried with Auntie Agatha at the time of the funeral. I will also have the exact location disguised, i.e., a secret reburial to protect from graverobbers. And I'll see to it that the will is admitted to probate forthwith. *(stiffly)* If any of you wish to dispute any term of the will, I suggest you see a lawyer. Good day.

Twoomey packs his briefcase and leaves, bowing at the door and closing it gently behind him.

CHARLIE: Well, that's it. To think that he too is one of our family.

KATE: *(stunned)* So the best part is to be buried with the old lady.

PEGG: Auntie Agatha put her whole life's savings into that golden pot and plant. She cheated us all. How she must be laughing at us.

GYPSY: I could never have foretold this disaster.

FRED: Oh dear, there are no rewards for education and ambition nowadays, the way there used to be in the good old days before the war. Oh how I wish that once again I was a happy gravedigger.

They begin to leave, slowly, bowed over and miserably. Lights begin to dim.

Curtain

ACT TWO - WHO GETS WHAT?

SCENE TWO

LIFE GOES ON

TIME: *After the funeral.*

SCENE: *Is the same, the lights are low and for a moment the stage is in darkness. Then, the closet containing the garden tools is opened, unseen to audience. Slowly, the spotlight picks out the closet picking out the spades and shovels conspicuously. There is a minute or so of pause as footsteps sound. No one is seen. The following voices are stage whispering and unrecognized.*

1ST VOICE: Tomorrow night? Not to desecrate the grave so soon after the funeral, right?

2ND VOICE: Naw - that would be too late. It would be gone by then.

1ST VOICE: Tonight then, right now?

2ND VOICE: You bet. You take a shovel. I'll take a spade.

1ST VOICE: *(softly)* Right. It's a deal - 50-50, equal shares?

2ND VOICE: Shake on it.

Spotlight remains on spades and shovels.
Sing: **GOLD BUGS**

GOLD BUGS

Sung: Jerkily and Cheerfully

VERSE 1:
d f l f d f l f
We shovel and slave, we rant and rave
d - d f f f m r m f s
As we scratch each patch for the wealth we crave
d f l f d f l f
Ho, ho, hee, hee, ho, ho, hee, hee
l d^1 l s s f
We'll bug all day for gold
d f l - l f d f l f
It's more than a joke, we've all gone broke
d f f - f - f m - r m - f s
It's not just a fad, we're raving mad
d f l f d f l f
Ho, ho, hee, hee, ho, ho, hee, hee
l d^1 l s s f
We'll bug all day for gold

VERSE 1:
We shovel and slave, we rant and rave
As we scratch each patch for the wealth we crave
Ho, ho, hee, hee, ho, ho, hee, hee
We'll bug all day for gold
It's more than a joke, we've all gone broke
It's not just a fad, we're raving mad
Ho, ho, hee, hee, ho, ho, hee, hee
We'll bug all day for gold.

REFRAIN:
Some little bugs come, some big bugs go
That's just the way of the world you know
But the only bugs who never grow old
Are the bugs who bug for gold
Smash up the stones, give them a kick
One more shovel load might do the trick
Ho, ho, hee, hee, ho, ho, hee, hee
We bug all day for gold.

VERSE 2:
And when we've found the gold we love
We'll bug some more for treasure trove
Ho, ho, hee, hee, ho, ho, hee, hee
We'll bug for treasure trove
The search for treasure never ends
We may strut all around and impress our friends
Ho, ho, hee, hee, ho, ho, hee, hee
Then we'll bug for treasure trove.

VERSE 3:
If you live in hope you'll never grow old
It'll keep you alive just a digging for gold
Ho, ho, hee, hee, ho, ho, hee, hee
We'll bug for silver and gold
But when we've made our very last try
We'll dig some more in the sweet bye and bye
Ho, ho, hee, hee, ho, ho, hee, hee
We're bugs for treasure trove.

Finale: All songs should now be repeated, whether sung or recited.

Curtain

END OF PLAYSCRIPT

DETECTIVES - ONLY JOKING?

A Short Story and a One-Act Play

The Story

It is a fact that some people take themselves too seriously as the following story illustrates.

In the downtown business district, where small business flourishes, there were a few small shops and offices as well as a few empty premises.

Lurking around, walking backward and forward, were four very professionally dressed young men and a glamorous southsea island model. Two of the young men were carrying cameras and the other two were dressed like plain-clothed detectives. Among the passers-by, striding manfully along the street, was a fat, well dressed but rather arrogant businessman carrying a briefcase and umbrella. He was middle-aged, well groomed, well dressed in business suit, glasses, shirt and tie and clean black shoes.

This city gent entered the sidewalk at a corner, with his head in the air. He strode out manfully but slowly along the street. He paused, produced a watch out of his waistcoat, consulted it, smiled in satisfaction - evidently he was on time - as he continued slowly along the street, humming and smiling to himself and yawning.

The two smartly dressed detectives approached the city gent, stopped him and showed him their IDs.

One of the detectives told him, "We're detectives from city police, Sir. Could we see your ID? We're in plain clothes."

The pretentious city gent produced his wallet and asked, "I can see that. But have I done anything wrong? My car is legally parked."

He then produced his ID/driver's license.

The second detective casually made a note of the puffed-up businessman's name and address. "Oh, no Sir. You've done nothing wrong at all Sir. It's just the opposite. You look like a first-class law-abiding businessman."

The first detective chipped in, "Yes, a respectable married man, right?"

The city gent was pleased and flattered, "Well, I suppose so but then why stop me here and ask me questions?"

One of the detectives looked around surreptitiously. "Respectable law abiding citizens are hard to come by these days - most folks are rogues around here . . what with City Hall and its politicians being near and Baptist Men's Mission around the corner and other such places of ill fame nearby."

The pretentious businessman smiled proudly, "Yes indeed, I pride myself on being a pillar of the business community. But why stop me of all people?"

One of the detectives pressed down the city gent's suit lapels flatteringly, "Why Sir, you would help us catch rogues who've been preying on honest businessmen like yourself, wouldn't you?"

The businessman heartily agreed, obviously flattered, "Why certainly. Matter of fact, if you'd like a good tip, I've always thought that Sherlock Holmes is rather a dull fellow compared to me."

"Just so," agreed the second detective. "But he didn't have your ah . . ." He looked at the be-suited city gent's large stomach, touched it lightly, then looked away . . "Your . . your acumen, Sir."

The businessman looked around and lowered his voice, "That's right officer . . however, you ought to be aware that he is a drug addict."

The detectives asked, "Who is?"

The eager businessman answered confidentially, "Why, Sherlock Holmes of course, whereas I never touch anything stronger than an aspirin."

One detective turned to the other and asked, "Where can we arrest this Sherlock Holmes suspect?"

The other detective shrugged, "Search me."

The snitching businessman eagerly supplied the needed information, "221B Baker Street, London, England that's where you'll catch the lawbreaker . . write it down, 221B Baker."

The second detective looked around anxiously, "Anyway Sir, that's a long way away. Much closer to home than way over there, you could help us catch a gang of scam artists and blackmailers and extortioners.

"Well, Sir, in this very street - see that sign up there 'Sharpeye Sam Photographer'." The police-loving businessman nodded eagerly. "Well, Sir, they're working a crude scam."

Then the businessman promised the detectives, "Well you can trust me to help you catch them. I pride myself on being a pillar of the business community."

The first detective was pleased, "All you have to do, Sir, is go along with their scam, pretend you believe it - can you pretend, Sir - just to trap them and ensnare them?"

The businessman laughed scornfully, "Pretend? Can I pretend, officers? Why, you should see me giving a sales presentation . . why I . . know what marketing and advertising is all about. I'm a smart businessman. Can I fake it? Can a cat drink milk?"

The detectives agreed, "That's all right, Sir. We believe you. Well, you need to pretend to be a victim but we can't arrest them under the law until their fraud is a fait accompli, that is to say, until they have taken your money. Then, when they've taken your money on false pretences - call us over – we'll be close by – we'll arrest them, return your cash, chuck them in the pen and forget where we threw the key O.K.?"

"O.K. But what is the scam?"

The detectives rubbed their chins ruminatively. "It could vary Sir, but its always some form of getting the victim into a compromising position - usually with a disreputable looking member of the opposite sex - taking a photograph of them - then threatening to send the photo to the victim's mother, or employer or wife - you know, it varies a little. Do you have an employer?"

The businessman replied, "No, I own my own business."

"Is your mother alive?"

"No, alas she passed away in Ireland many years ago. It was in the winter in the snow. I was so sorry; it was so cold for her funeral."

"But you are married Sir?"

"Certainly."

"Then that will probably be their track. Threatening to send the photos to your wife - or a rich uncle who is writing his will or a main customer or to your doting elderly wealthy aunt, most likely. Yes, that would probably be their approach - but anyway they do it, it's still blackmail and extortion if they want money in return for not sending the photos to anyone. See?"

"Right - the scoundrels."

The detectives concluded, "Well Sir, we'll retreat to the corner - we will be keeping you under observation. As soon as the money changes hands - give us the nod and we'll nab them. All right Sir?

"By the way, there's a 12,000 reward for catching these crooks but, I'm sorry Sir, Al and I have worked so long on finding these scam artists - that reward would have to be split three ways - tentatively, that is if that's O.K. with you Sir. After all, we have families to support and you would still get 4,000."

The businessman was delighted and beamed, "Certainly, certainly officers. I've no objection to sharing the reward with you. Fair is fair."

The two detectives nodded respectfully and moved to the street corner where they posed in casual conversation but kept an eye on the subsequent events.

The swaggering businessman cleared his throat, squared his shoulders, straightened his tie, feigned innocence and strutted towards the doorway of Sharpeye Sam. He walked past it. Nothing happened. He looked around, puzzled, scratched his head and then walked on.

The other two young men then approached the snobbish businessman, whom they asked, "Oh yes, Sir. Did I see you looking at our sign?" They pointed to the shop known as Sharpeye Sam, Photographer, "I'm sorry we were out to lunch. You need some photos? Yes?

"We can help you. What kind of photos do you need? Passport, I.D., holiday?

"How about a holiday, weekend photo to show around the office. High status - holiday weekend to impress your colleagues or employees. They'll take you for a highly successful millionaire having great fun on weekends."

The smug city gent waved to police officers, who nodded and encouraged him, as he told the photographers, "Oh yes. Well, why not, eh?"

Then the photographers ushered the businessman through the door of Sharpeye Sam's. It was opened by a beautiful southsea beauty dressed in swimwear and grass skirt.

"Yes, Sir. How about a Hawaiian special, O.K? You need to look successful, a big success."

The businessman looked dubiously at the police who nodded and turned away.

The self-important city gent replied, "Oh yes. Why not? A little extra status and success wouldn't hurt me with the old customers."

They all removed some outer clothing as passers-by fled in horror.

One of the photographers was very enthusiastic, "Well, let's get a good pose. Here Wackula, you slink around our esteemed friend's shoulder there and help him to succeed. Here, pose against this travel poster here in the window."

Wackula, the southsea island beauty, hung closely to the conceited businessman and gazed into his eyes. She kissed his cheek as he held her close and smiled for the photographer. Several flash photos were taken as they continued to remove outer clothing.

The photographers assiduously checked their equipment, pretending to make sure the photos were an instant good print-out success. They looked at the photos, nodded to each other with approval and asked the businessman, "Yes, very compromising. This will be five for photographs. O.K?"

But the businessman was puzzled, "Only five. Oh sure, here you are." He counted out the money.

The photographers pocketed the money and told the businessman, "Sir, that's fine. We'll send it to your home address when it's all fully developed in multi-color."

Then the city gent began to get rattled, put back on his outer clothes, stepped back out of the door and beckoned to the two detectives, who did not notice him or respond.

The businessman cried out, "Hey, just a minute. My wife opens my mail. You can't do that!"

One of the photographers replied confidentially, "It's all right. No worry. We mark the envelope - *Confidential Photos not to be opened by unauthorized persons*."

But the rattled businessman was still desperately trying to attract the attention of the detectives. "You must be crazy . . that would only make her certain to open it. She opens everything that says - confidential."

The two photographers began to laugh and chortle, "Dear, dear, what a wife! How unusual! Curiosity killed the cat. Ha, ha, ha – except that you happen to be the cat – ha, ha, ha."

Wackula joined in the laughter, "Oh, I wouldn't want you to get into trouble with your wife just because of a funny photo with silly old me. We can sell you the photos and film right now on an emergency basis. No problem, just 500."

The businessman placed his hand to head and nodded, "Oh yes. Of course. Heck, I only have 477." He offered them the money and they accepted it.

They bowed respectfully as the businessman handed over the money and replaced the empty wallet in his inside pocket and accepted the photos. He signaled the two detectives and clearly beckoned them to join him.

The two detectives quickly approached, coolly and curiously as the cleaned-out, ripped-off businessman cried out, "Just a minute. On second thoughts, I want my money back. You can't send the photos to my wife. You don't have my address. Police officers! Come here! At once!"

The second photographer bowed again and replied respectfully, "No, but the detectives only joking have your address."

The extortioned businessman was astonished, "So what?" He addressed the detectives, "Arrest these scoundrels! Get me my money back."

The detectives shook their heads, "But why should we arrest these good kin of ours – this is our cousin Tom, our cousin Dick and our most beautiful cousin Wackula."

Tom, Dick and Wackula all laughed. "Why should we arrest them?"

Then the photographers enlightened the demonetized businessman. "It's all a joke. The joke is on you. We are all friends and we keep the 500. That is 100 each."

"We are Detectives Only Joking. We are the Pretend Police."

The businessman slouched home a little less arrogantly.

Well, it all just goes to show that you can't believe one half of the lies you hear and the other half probably aren't even true.

However, on the subject of the eager informant, a lot of people take themselves too seriously. They imagine that the big money they are earning is all, but all, because of their hard work and their shrewdness.

Of course, training and good decisions are a part of success but not by any means the whole story. Well beyond the control of any individual are the wars, revolutions, riots, epidemics, laws, booms and busts, fashions and trends.

So it comes about that some folk are the fortunate children of luck. Their fate was spun at birth on the wheel of destiny. They need to know that a lucky man needs only to be born and that is not much of an achievement. These lucky people need to have more humility so that they can appreciate that good fortune is the result of a random walk down Business Street.

END OF STORY

The Playscript

PRODUCTION NOTES

ONE SET

A city street, the same in all scenes.

ACTORS

Seven actors. The uniformed police officer and two photographers may be male or female. The scam perpetrators should speak with phony accents.

STAGE TIME

Approximately half an hour

MUSIC

One song: *Dress a Little Less*

OUTLINE OF THE PLAY

SCENE ONE:

A Pompous Businessman

SCENE TWO:

All to Help the Police

SCENE THREE:

Don't Tell my Wife

CHARACTERS IN THE PLAY

POMPOUS BUSINESSMAN -

A stroller along a busy street

1ST DETECTIVE AND 2ND DETECTIVE -

Phony policemen in league with three other small-time crooks

1ST PHOTOGRAPHER AND 2ND PHOTOGRAPHER -

Two petty confidence tricksters

WACKULA -
A glamorous model (may be oriental or Hawaiian)
OTHER - A regular uniformed police officer.

****

SCENE ONE - A POMPOUS BUSINESSMAN

The scene is a dimly lit street in the downtown area of any large city. Along the backdrop area stretching almost the full length of stage is a brick wall broken by doorways and a few small windows. Above one doorway is a sign 'Go Come Imports' and beside another door is 'Sharpeye Sam Photographer.' One of the other doors leads to a travel agents. In front of all this is a paved sidewalk.

Right and left is scenery depicting cars in the distance as of an adjacent road. At each end of the wall is a corner where the sidewalk winds round and out of sight. At extreme right on sidewalk is a mailbox. At extreme left is a street lamp - perhaps an old fashioned one for period effect, although the period (1950s, 70s, 90s) is not important. However, cars and costumes should be of approximately the same period. This is a respectable part of the downtown business district where small business flourishes.

Any reasonable number of extras may walk past in either direction, all well dressed as business men and women and carrying such appropriate props as umbrellas, walking sticks, briefcases, mobile phones (if the period chosen permits).

The general impression is of a busy, respectable but somewhat of a minor or side street, small business area, downtown.

***Enter from left, four young men** who light-heartedly ask the passers-by for some fish and chips. Passers-by laugh and pay little attention. The four are later identified as 1st and 2nd Detective and 1st and 2nd Photographer.*

***Enter from right, Wackula,** carrying a camera and wearing bikini and grass skirt.*

1st DETECTIVE: Wackula, where are you off to - a movie part?

WACKULA: No, just a photo session.

2nd DETECTIVE: Buy us all a fish and chips?

WACKULA: No, got no dough.

1st PHOTOGRAPHER: Does that camera work?

WACKULA: No, it's just a prop. They'll put me in front of a screen painted with coconut trees and I'll pose as a tourist for a travel company ad, like those in the window there.

2nd PHOTOGRAPHER: That gives me an idea. Can you hang around one of these shops for a minute, until I find a benefactor for all of us? Remember the play we did in the drama club - "Detectives only Joking?"

WACKULA: Sure - the pretend police. *(she enters one of the shops - a travel agents)*

Enter from left Pompous Businessman, *fat, middle-aged, well groomed, well dressed in business suit, glasses, shirt and tie, clean black shoes, carrying a briefcase and umbrella. He enters the sidewalk at left corner and, head in air, struts pompously, but slowly along street. He pauses, produces watch out of his waistcoat or inside pocket, consults it, smiles in satisfaction - evidently he is on time - as he continues slowly and pompously along street, humming and smiling to himself and yawning.*

Approach from right two detectives. *The detectives should be weird characters with beards, funny hair styles, odd clothes and with a strange way of speaking (e.g., very slow or fast and stuttering). They are unlikely to be real detectives, yet the naive but Pompous Businessman believes them. The two poorly dressed detectives (may be male or female) approach Pompous Businessman, stop him and show their IDs.*

1st DETECTIVE: We're detectives from city police, Sir. Could we see your ID. *(Pompous Businessman produces wallet)* We're in plain clothes.

POMPOUS BUSINESSMAN: *(in disgust)* I can see that. But have I done anything wrong? My car is legally parked. *(he produces his ID/driver's license)*

2nd DETECTIVE: *(making a note of Pompous Businessman's name and address, casually)* Oh, no Sir. You've done nothing wrong at all Sir. It's just the opposite. You look like a first-class law-abiding businessman.

1st DETECTIVE: Yes, a respectable married man, right.

POMPOUS BUSINESSMAN: Well *(pleased and flattered)* I suppose so, but then why stop me here and ask me questions?

2nd DETECTIVE: *(looking around surreptitiously)* Respectable law abiding citizens are hard to come by these days - most folks are rogues around here . . what with City Hall being near and Baptist Men's Mission around the corner and other such places of ill fame nearby.

POMPOUS BUSINESSMAN: Yes indeed, I pride myself on being a pillar of the business community. But why stop me of all people?

1st DETECTIVE: *(pressing down the Pompous Businessman's suit lapels flatteringly)* Why Sir, you would help us catch rogues who've been preying on honest businessmen like yourself, wouldn't you?

POMPOUS BUSINESSMAN: Why certainly. *(flattered)* Matter of fact, if you'd like a good tip, I've always thought that Sherlock Holmes is rather a dull fellow compared to me.

2nd DETECTIVE: Just so. He didn't have your ah . . *(looks at Pompous Businessman's stomach, touches it lightly, then looks away)* . . your . . your acumen, Sir.

POMPOUS BUSINESSMAN: That's right officer and *(looking around)* however, you ought to be aware that he is a drug addict.

1st DETECTIVE: Who is?

POMPOUS BUSINESSMAN: *(as one giving confidential information in a stage whisper)* Why, Sherlock Holmes of course, whereas I never touch anything stronger than an aspirin.

2nd DETECTIVE: *(to 1st Detective)* Where can we arrest this Sherlock Holmes suspect?

1st DETECTIVE: *(shaking head and spreading out hands)* Search me.

POMPOUS BUSINESSMAN: *(eagerly)* 221B Baker Street, London, England that's where you'll catch the lawbreaker . . write it down, 221B Baker.

2nd DETECTIVE: *(looking around anxiously)* Anyway Sir, that's a long way away. Much closer to home than way over there, you could help us catch a gang of scam artists and blackmailers and extortioners.

POMPOUS BUSINESSMAN: I'm always happy to co-operate with the law. As a matter of fact, there's *(confidentially)* a very suspicious house near where I live *(looking over his shoulder)* let me tell you what those weirdoes are up to . . .

1st DETECTIVE: *(interrupting)* Later, Sir. Later. As for now - look - can we trust you with confidential information?

POMPOUS BUSINESSMEN: Who me? I assure you I've never been known to gossip. *(adamantly)* I've never been known to blab or squeal. My integrity, Sirs, is *(pompously)* unimpeachable. Why, Officers, I've never snitched on anyone.

1st DETECTIVE: Except Sherlock Holmes. *(laughs and pats him on the shoulder)*

POMPOUS BUSINESSMAN: Ah, *(seriously)* but he really is a drugger.

2nd DETECTIVE: *(breaking in)* Quite, Quite. Well, Sir, in this very street - see that sign 'Sharpeye Sam Photographer'. *(Pompous Businessman nods eagerly)* Well, Sir, they're working a crude scam.

POMPOUS BUSINESSMAN: *(scared and aghast)* No. No. You don't say? . . . Surely not!

2nd Detective nods significantly.

1st DETECTIVE: *(raising his head)* My right hand up.

POMPOUS BUSINESSMAN: Well you can trust me to help you catch them. I pride myself on being a pillar of the business community.

2nd DETECTIVE: *(looking at the Pompous Businessman's protruding stomach and lightly touching his lower lapel)* Well . . hmm yes, Sir . . you seem to be quite a, well, solid citizen.

POMPOUS BUSINESSMAN: *(smugly and oblivious)* Thank you, Officer.

1st DETECTIVE: All you have to do, Sir, is go along with their scam, pretend you believe it - can you pretend, Sir - just to trap them and ensnare them?

POMPOUS BUSINESSMAN: Pretend? Can I pretend, officers? *(he laughs)* Why you should see me giving a sales presentation . . why I . . know what marketing and advertising is all about. I'm a businessman.

1st DETECTIVE: That's all right, Sir. We believe you. *(2nd detective nods)* Well, you need to pretend to be a victim but we can't arrest them under the law until their fraud is a fait accompli *(Pompous Businessman looks blank)* that is to say, until they have taken your money. Then, when they've taken your money on false pretences - call us over – we'll be close by – we'll arrest them, return your cash, chuck them in the pen and forget where we threw the key O.K.?

POMPOUS BUSINESSMAN: O.K. But what is the scam?

1st DETECTIVE: *(rubbing his chin ruminatively)* It could vary Sir, but its always some form of getting the victim into a compromising position - usually with a disreputable looking member of the opposite sex - taking a photograph of them - then threatening to send the photo to the victim's mother, or employer or wife - you know, it varies a little. Do you have an employer?

POMPOUS BUSINESSMAN: No, I own my own business.

1st DETECTIVE: Is your mother alive?

POMPOUS BUSINESSMAN: No, alas she passed away in Ireland many years ago. It was in the winter in the snow.

2nd DETECTIVE: *(interrupting)* But you are married?

POMPOUS BUSINESSMAN: Certainly.

1st DETECTIVE: Then that will probably be their track. Threatening to send the photos to your wife - or a rich uncle who is writing his will or a main customer or to your doting elderly wealthy aunt, most likely. *(nods reflectively)* Yes, that would probably be their approach - but anyway they do it, it's still blackmail and extortion if they want money in return for <u>not</u> sending the photos to anyone. See?

POMPOUS BUSINESSMAN: Right - the scoundrels!

2nd DETECTIVE: Well Sir, we'll retreat to the corner - we will be keeping you under observation. As soon as the money changes hands - give us the nod and we'll nab them. All right Sir?

POMPOUS BUSINESSMAN: You can depend on me. I'm a pretty good actor you know. In the school drama I acted the part of Polonius in . . .

2nd DETECTIVE: *(interrupting)* By the way, there's a 12,000 reward for catching these crooks but, I'm sorry Sir, Al and I have worked so long on finding these scam artists - that reward would have to be split three ways - tentatively, that is if that's O.K. with you Sir. After all, we have families to support and you would still get 4,000.

POMPOUS BUSINESSMAN: *(delighted and beaming)* Certainly, certainly officers. I've no objection to sharing the reward with you. Fair is fair.

The two detectives nod respectfully and move to the street corner left where they pose in casual conversation but keep an eye on the subsequent events.

Curtain

SCENE TWO – ALL TO HELP THE POLICE

The same as before. Pompous Businessman is still on stage. Pompous Businessman clears his throat, squares his shoulders, straightens his tie and, feigning innocence, struts towards the doorway of Sharpeye Sam. He walks past it. Nothing happens. He looks around, puzzled, scratches his head then walks on.

Two photographers enter right *along the sidewalk and approach Pompous Businessman.*

These photographers are flashy and cheaply dressed much like the detectives but with such variation as wide padded shoulders and bright tie, suit and white shoes, in fact - very flaky characters in contrast to the quiet, respectably dressed businessman.

1st PHOTOGRAPHER: *(to Pompous Businessman)* Oh yes, Sir. Did I see you looking at our sign? I'm sorry we were out to lunch. You need some photos?

2nd PHOTOGRAPHER: We can help you. What kind of photos do you need? Passport, I.D., Holiday?

1st PHOTOGRAPHER: How about a holiday, weekend photo to show around the office. *(Pompous Businessman is puzzled)* High status - holiday weekend to impress your colleagues or employees. Take you for a highly successful millionaire having great fun on weekends.

Pompous Businessman waves to police officers, who nod and encourage him.

POMPOUS BUSINESSMAN: *(understanding a little better now)* Oh yes. Well, why not, eh?

1st Photographer knocks door of Sharpeye Sam's. It is opened by a beautiful southsea beauty dressed in swimwear and grass skirt.

2nd PHOTOGRAPHER: Yes, Sir. How about a Hawaiian special, O.K? *(to Pompous Businessman)* You need to look successful, a big success.

ALL: *They sing* ***DRESS A LITTLE LESS*** *throughout the routine.*

DRESS A LITTLE LESS

Sung: Fast and Funny

VERSE 1:

s m - m - m f
Dress a little less
r d t_1 - s_1
For more success
l_1 d - d - d r d m
Dress a little less for more
m s m f
More sun more fun
r d - t_1 s_1
More prizes won
s_1 l_1 d - d - d - d d t_1 d
If you dress a little less for more

VERSE 1:
Dress a little less
For more success
Dress a little less for more
More sun more fun
More prizes won
If you dress a little less for more.

VERSE 2:
Dress a little less
Get more caress
And glance and dance galore
Less dress excess
Means more success
So dress a little less for more

VERSE 3:
Dress a little less
For more success
Dress a little less for more
More lass, more class
More lads with brass
Dress a little less for more.

VERSE 4:
Dress a little less
For more success
Dress a little less for more
More flash, more bash
More seaside brash
Dress a little less for more.

VERSE 5:
Dress a little less
Get more caress
And glance and dance galore
Less dress excess
Means more success
If you dress a little less for more.

Pompous Businessman looks at police dubiously. They nod and turn away.

POMPOUS BUSINESSMAN: Oh yes. Why not. A little extra status and success wouldn't hurt me with the old customers. *(they all remove some outer clothing as passers-by flee in horror)*

1st PHOTOGRAPHER: Well, let's get a good pose. Here Wackula, you slink around our esteemed friend's shoulder there and help him to succeed. Here, pose against this travel poster here in the window.

Wackula, the southsea island beauty, hangs closely to Pompous Businessman and gazes into his eyes. She kisses his cheek as he holds her close and smiles for the photographer. Several flash photos are taken as they continue to remove outer clothing.

Enter the uniformed police officer.

UNIFORMED POLICE OFFICER: Stop! That's quite enough.

Uniformed police officer leaves stage.

The photographers assiduously check their equipment pretending to make sure the photos are an instant good print-out success. They look at the supposed photos and nod to each other and approve. They finish the song.

1st PHOTOGRAPHER: *(to Pompous Businessman)* Yes, very compromising. This will be 5 for photographs. O.K.

POMPOUS BUSINESSMAN: *(puzzled)* Only 5. Oh sure, here you are. *(pays it)*

2nd PHOTOGRAPHER: *(taking the 5)* Sir, that's fine. We'll send it to your home address when it's all fully developed in multi-color.

POMPOUS BUSINESSMAN: *(getting rattled, putting back on his outer clothing and beckoning to the two detectives, who do not notice him or respond)* Hey, just a minute. My wife opens my mail. You can't do that!

1st PHOTOGRAPHER: Oh *(confidentially)* It's all right. No worry. We mark the envelope "Confidential Photos not to be opened by unauthorized persons."

POMPOUS BUSINESSMAN: *(desperately trying to attract attention of detectives)* But that would only make her certain to open it. She opens everything that says "confidential."

1st AND 2nd PHOTOGRAPHERS: *(laughing)* Dear, dear, what a wife! How unusual! Curiosity killed the cat. Ha, ha, ha - except that you happen to be the cat - ha, ha, ha. *(they chortle)*

WACKULA: Oh, I wouldn't want you to get into trouble with your wife just because of a funny photo with silly old me. We can sell you the photos and film right now on an emergency basis. No problem.

POMPOUS BUSINESSMAN: *(relieved)* Really?

WACKULA: Of course. We want to help you. *(to others)* Can't you do this dear fellow a favor boys.

1st AND 2nd PHOTOGRAPHER: Oh, yes. Yes, most certainly. Emergency service. Photos on the spot, negatives and all - no follow up, sales, no enlargements, no use of film in contests or professional photographer magazines or newspapers - just a once and for all time all-in-all - rights and full copyright of all films - naturally more expensive - just 500. *(they nod helpfully)*

POMPOUS BUSINESSMAN: *(incredulous)* 500. *(he looks in desperation at detectives. They nod vigorously and place hands together as for cufflinks and nod towards the three scam artists)*

POMPOUS BUSINESSMAN: *(placing hand to head and nodding)* Oh yes. Of course. *(to Wackula and two photographers)* Sure *(gulp)* no problem. Oh yes 500. Yes, it's worth it. Gee, my wife could make real trouble for me. *(brings out wallet and counts out money)* Heck, I only have 477. *(he offers it)*

WACKULA: Oh yes, honey. *(nodding to the two photographers)* That's near enough. Isn't it?

TWO PHOTOGRAPHERS: Sure. Near enough. *(they take the money)* Sure, fine. No point in being picky. If that's all you have, who are we to argue. *(they laugh and chortle)* Thank you, Sir. We appreciate your business.

They bow respectfully as Pompous Businessman hands over the money and replaces the empty wallet in his inside pocket and accepts the photos. He signals the two detectives and clearly beckons them to his side.

<u>Curtain</u>

SCENE THREE – DON'T TELL MY WIFE

Same. All on stage as before. The two detectives quickly approach coolly and curiously.

POMPOUS BUSINESSMAN: Just a minute. On second thoughts, I want my money back. You can't send the photos to my wife. You don't have my address. Police officers! Come here! At once!

2nd PHOTOGRAPHER: No, but the detectives only joking have your address.

POMPOUS BUSINESSMAN: So what?

1st DETECTIVE: What's going on here?

2nd DETECTIVE: *(looking the others over)* I think there's a call for some explanation here.

The two detectives show their IDs to all present, prominently, conspicuously and step back authoritatively.

1st DETECTIVE: All right, you three rogues *(to the two photographers and Wackula)* talk, tell this businessman what it's all about!

1st PHOTOGRAPHER: *(reading from Detective #1's ID card)* Well done!

2nd PHOTOGRAPHER: *(reading from Detective #2's ID card)* Good Job!

POMPOUS BUSINESSMAN: *(confused)* What's up? What's wrong? What's the problem?

All others laugh and chortle.

WACKULA: Nothing up. Nothing wrong. No problem.

PHOTOGRAPHERS AND THE DETECTIVES: *(laughing)* Nothing up. Everything fine. Everybody happy.

POMPOUS BUSINESSMAN: Very well. *(to detectives)* Arrest these scoundrels! Get me my money back.

1st DETECTIVE: What charge?

2nd DETECTIVE: *(outraged)* Arrest them?

POMPOUS BUSINESSMAN: Certainly, just as we arranged. They conned me out of 500.

1st DETECTIVE: But why should I arrest these good kin of mine – this is my cousin Tom, my cousin Dick and my most beautiful cousin Wackula. *(Tom, Dick and Wackula all laugh)* Why should I arrest them?

POMPOUS BUSINESSMAN: *(to Tom, Dick and Wackula)* But what's the joke. You three are all going to be arrested. *(then to detectives)* Cousins or no cousins. Aren't they? Why are they laughing?

1st PHOTOGRAPHER: It's all a joke.

POMPOUS BUSINESSMAN: *(confused)* What's a joke? Where's the joke?

2nd PHOTOGRAPHER: The joke is on <u>you</u>.

POMPOUS BUSINESSMAN: Oh, I see. It's only a joke. Oh, I get it. *(he laughs heartily)* Yes, it's only a joke – I see – ha, ha, ha. *(sobering and feeling for his wallet)* Oh, I do appreciate a joke. O.K. if you'll just give me back my 500 or 477 or whatever I'll be on my way. I am in a hurry. I have important clients to see.

WACKULA: *(insidiously and slinkingly)* You mean clients like your dear deranged wife. Oh, I'll deal with her for you.

POMPOUS BUSINESSMAN: *(to detectives)* What's going on here? I demand that you arrest these scoundrels, get back my photos and my money. Come on, you're servants of the taxpayer. *(all others laugh)* You're detectives. *(hesitating as the others all laugh)* Aren't you? Aren't you?

1st DETECTIVE: Ha, ha. Detectives only joking. We're family photographers. We have your address. We have the photos. We have your 500. We have the lot and we keep it. If you go to the real police, your wife will get a visit from Wackula, who has a confession to make and photos to back it up. Ah, ah. What a scandal!

POMPOUS BUSINESSMAN: *(confused)* But I don't understand. I did this to help out the law.

WACKULA: Nobody would believe that story . . what a tall tale. *(she covers her mouth with her hand and giggles)*

POMPOUS BUSINESSMAN: *(doubtfully to detectives)* So you're not police. You're criminals. This is a crime! A con trick.

2nd DETECTIVE: No, no. Can't you take a joke – a little fun? This is not a confidence trick. Small amount of money concerned. Sense of humor is good. We are detectives only joking.

Detectives Only Joking?

All except Pompous Businessman laugh hilariously. ***Pompous Businessman walks off, right-stage,*** *shaking his head and looking back in anger, fear and distrust. He waves down his hand at the others in a sad and sorry farewell.*

TOM, DICK AND WACKULA AND THE TWO DETECTIVES: *(in unison after departure of Pompous Businessman)* Detectives!! Detectives!! Ah, ha, ha.
(pathetically holding out their hands in a gesture of hopelessness)
Detectives only joking. The Pretend Police.

1st DETECTIVE: Ha, Ha, Ha. Camera doesn't even work. Ho, Ho.

2nd DETECTIVE: This money is burning a hole. What can we spend it on?

WACKULA: Even Sharpeye Sam has been closed for six months. Let's get outa here.

Repeat song.

Curtain

END OF PLAYSCRIPT

SORE BOTTOM

A Short Story and a
Three-Act Mime imitating
a Black and White Silent Movie

The Story

It is funny how a human life can be affected in many different facets by one irrelevant, even random, event. TerryBill Sohrbottom had a sore bottom. Whether this was for a little while, or a long time, is not clear. However, it affected his entire life - socially, romantically, religiously, jobwise and certainly his capital position. The reason for TerryBill's sore bottom whether hereditary, dietary or socially is not relevant. Perhaps it was just a reaction to cold weather. At any rate, TerryBill's first stop, foolishly, was to visit a doctor and to ask for some medicine.

"Doc, I have a sore bottom." He blurted out.

The doctor was outraged at what he saw as being an attack on his professional integrity. "How dare you diagnose yourself, you brat. That is my job. I'll tell you whether or not you have a sore bottom."

When TerryBill persisted in his complaint, the doctor flew into a rage and ordered him out of his office.

As TerryBill limped out in some pain, the doctor continued to rant and rave, "There's no respect for professionalism these days," he hollered, shaking his fist after the departing TerryBill.

Scarcely noticing that a new patient had entered his office, a prim and sedate old lady with a cold, he stabbed his stethoscope into the air, "I'd like to hit you where it hurts most," he yelled, and stuck the stethoscope on the old lady's posterior. She screamed in terror and ran out of the office, calling for the police.

Realizing his blunder, the doctor calmed down and ran after the old lady apologizing profusely but it was too late. He had lost another patient due to his arrogance and contempt for humanity.

Seeing that his visit to the doctor had been such a disaster, TerryBill strolled into the nearest restaurant to relax. Naturally, he chose not to sit down but rather stood at the bar and ordered a coffee. Two young ladies were sitting nearby engaged in pleasant and relaxed conversation. TerryBill offered to buy them coffees and they accepted, motioning him to join them at a nearby chair. TerryBill remembered that he could not sit down and had to decline politely, raising his hat and continuing to stand at the counter. After a while, the young ladies left politely thanking TerryBill for the coffee. TerryBill was at a loss what to do and decided to pay a visit to his uncle's place of work.

His uncle was pleased to see him, showed TerryBill over his small factory, and invited TerryBill to sit down. Unable to do so, TerryBill squirmed about and finally propped himself up on his elbow on a nearby shelf.

The uncle began to tell TerryBill that the business was flourishing and announced that he could offer TerryBill a white-collar managerial position as the marketing director. After thinking about this carefully, TerryBill felt that he had to decline this offer and to ask for a manual position as a painter instead. The uncle was quite offended at the idea of TerryBill avoiding responsibility and opting for a low level routine position. "You will never get anywhere by doing simple tasks and evading difficult and creative work. I'm afraid I can do nothing for you, TerryBill."

TerryBill limped away towards the town center, still hobbling around and leaning on various supports such as car hoods, prams, motorbikes and the like.

By now TerryBill was becoming tired and felt the need to either sit down or lie down. There was no opportunity for either of these means of respite so he continued to struggle on shakily. Finally, he came to an outdoor gospel meeting, where everyone was standing to sing. Gratefully, he joined the crowd and was given a hymn book by one of the members of the group. Although he was still in great pain, he enjoyed the singing which took his mind off his discomfort. Abruptly, however, the singing came to an end and everyone sat down on extemporaneous benches. Everyone, that is, except TerryBill, who continued to move uncomfortably from one leg to another as the preacher began to wave his bible at the crowd.

The preacher pointed to heaven and then to the earth, "Everyone who wishes to join us, stand up," he entreated.

This invitation was to be one of the highlights of the sermon.

TerryBill, still in great pain, shouted out, "I cannot stand up any longer."

Noticing that TerryBill was the only person standing, the preacher joyfully beckoned TerryBill to come forward. After TerryBill had cheerfully agreed to join the happy band up yonder, he was welcomed and accepted by several members of the congregation including the soloist, a beautiful young lady called Mavis, whom TerryBill soon fell in love with.

After a few days of courtship, they became engaged and TerryBill was invited to visit her father's farm. She was an only child and her father was looking for help around the farm.

Her father was not too pleased when TerryBill pointed out that he could not milk the cows as this required sitting on a stool. Likewise, the old man was disappointed when TerryBill admitted that he could not drive the farm van on its house-to-house round of eggs, milk and vegetables.

"Sorry, Paw," said TerryBill, "but I can do other things. In fact, both Mavis and I can help out at mowing the grass, picking berries and vegetables. I don't mind walking alongside the old Clydesdales – there's a few good years left in them. Matter of fact, I can paint the walls, cut the hedges and collect the eggs."

Mavis' father was well pleased, "Well," he agreed, "we can all be partners and you two can take over when I retire."

TerryBill's losses were his arrogant doctor, his social coffee drinking and a job with his uncle but he was set up in his happy marriage, his church membership and his partnership in a farm - all just by suffering from sore bottom.

It is not known how long the sore bottom lasted but, short or long-term, the effects were certainly lifelong. What a strange world we live in. What a funny life!

END OF STORY

Sore Bottom

The Playscript

A MIME IN THREE ACTS - RECREATING A BLACK AND WHITE SILENT MOVIE

GENERAL STAGE INSTRUCTIONS

Most of the stage scenery for this play's short scenes can be presented on backdrops or on one to three screens of cardboard or wood. If screens are used, one simple method is to paint the scenery on the blank side of rolls of wallpaper. The painted strips are lined up together and pinned or taped in place.

Alternatively, large blank poster cards can be painted and pinned in sections to the screens in between scenes - the larger the cards the less time it will take to change scenes. Of course, the producer may elect to use more costly and sophisticated methods such as roll on - roll off stage furniture, and/or stage-wide painted canvas or textile curtains dropped and raised on a fly but such can be expensive in time and money.

All scenery is in black and white only. The actors in this innovative mime are to represent characters in an early 20th century silent movie. All their movements are jerky and delivered in the highly exaggerated melodramatic fashion of the genre. At intervals, explanation cards are carried across the stage, held for a few seconds to be read by the audience and then carried off stage. The actors carrying these reading cards should be smiling and pleasant. Cards should be printed in large clear old-fashioned letters, preferably capitals.

The accompanying piano music, if any, is selected by the stage director and should be racy and highlighted by sudden stops and runs at the main points of the action. If pre-recorded and played on tape, there will, of course, be co-ordination needed for the music to line-up with the action, for which reason a live pianist is always preferable.

All quoted speech is silent, but as clearly lip mimed as possible, in order to facilitate lip reading on the part of the audience.

As in all mime, everyday gestures are greatly exaggerated. Bows are as low as is physically possible; head shakes are vigorous; hand shakes are a swift series of highs and lows; nods of agreement are intense exercises in head-bobbing with wide smiles and so on. Early black and white movies were based on mime because of the absence of speech. Some brief episodes are played backwards as the 'reel' temporarily flies into reverse.

OUTLINE OF THE PLAY

ACT ONE - A YOUNG MAN'S TROUBLES

Scene One: Oh Doctor, Oh Doctor

ACT TWO - REJECTION

Scene One: Demon Rum

Scene Two: Uncle's Factory

ACT THREE – A FORTUNATE MEETING

Scene One: Standing Ovation

Scene Two: But Father is a Hard Man
Scene Three: A Job for TerryBill
Scene Four: A Sore but Happy End

PRODUCTION SPECIFICATIONS

SCENERY - FOUR SETS:

Doctor's Office
The Strand Cafe (twice)
Uncle's Office
Farm of Mr Workacre
Three acts in seven scenes

STAGE TIME: About 1.1/2 hours
SEASON: Summer
TIMESPAN: A few days
ACTORS: 17 actors - 10 male, 7 female
Several extras as background figures, visiting the cafe, the strand, the bandstand area, father's farm
TIME: Various times of day
PLACE: A fashionable seaside resort
PERIOD AND COSTUMES: Late 19th or early 20th century
MUSIC: All music and songs should be played in the background and off-stage by a group of four or more. Five songs. *Drink Your Tea, Fish and Chips, Food Ain't as Good, the Swallow Song, What a Good Dog.*
AGE GROUPS: All ages of audiences. Late teens to mature older for actors.
For radio or audiotape productions a narrator will be needed. Here the speech that is mimed in the visual version would, of course, be spoken.

THE MAIN CHARACTERS

DR. ROARER - a bad-tempered, nasty general practitioner.

TERRYBILL SOHRBOTTOM - an aristocratic young gentleman.

LADY ELEGANT - a young gentlewoman, well dressed, bright and beautiful.

BARTENDER - deaf and suspicious.

TWO YOUNG LADIES - also out wining and dining.

UNCLE MAKEM SOHRBOTTOM - proud owner of a furniture manufacturing company.

FAT MAN - with a bass drum.

SMALL SKINNY WOMAN - with an accordion.

TALL SKINNY MAN - with a trumpet.

FAT WOMAN - with a trombone.

PREACHER - with a large black book.

TALL THIN MAN - a witness.

SMALL FAT WOMAN - a witness.

MAVIS - a girl singer.

FARMER WORKACRE - the father of Mavis.

****

ACT ONE - A YOUNG MAN'S TROUBLES

SCENE ONE:

OH DOCTOR, OH DOCTOR

A doctor's office. Walls are lined with thick learned books, glasses, bottles, vials, charts, scales, anatomical specimens such as hands, feet, spines, skulls, skeletons. (All these may be props or painted on a backdrop or screens, see general stage instructions) All are in black and white only, as is everything on stage.

Doctor Roarer sits on a swivel chair at a large desk, left center, engrossed in paperwork. He is large, fat, villainous-looking with thick glasses and a full faced beard. He is white collared, black tied and dressed in a heavy gray tweed suit with waistcoat and chain, solid black boots and thick woolen white socks. Over his suit he wears an open white coat and stethoscope. The doctor bends forward and straightens up rapidly over his desk, left of center, reading and writing. At times he places a hand on his chin or head in contemplation.

Right of center there is a long couch. Close by the doctor there is a patient's chair.

***Enter TerryBill Sohrbottom**, slim, tall, clean shaven in white suit, black waistcoat, tie and shoes, white straw hat with a black band. He is* *naturally elegant, but limps occasionally and sometimes touches his rear-end tenderly. He carries a black walking stick with a white handle. He taps on the wall of the doctor's office, near the entrance. He presents an uncomfortable but aristocratic appearance.*

DOCTOR: *(without looking up)* Come in, come in.

TerryBill hesitates.

DOCTOR: *(irritably)* Oh come in. *(he beckons widely with his left hand without lifting his eyes from his desk)*

TerryBill enters tentatively.

DOCTOR: *(still not looking up and gesturing twice to chair)* Sit down, sit down.

TerryBill tiptoes over to chair, looks at it dubiously, draws back from it in fear, touches his bottom and jumps.

DOCTOR: *(repeating his former gesture twice more)* Sit down, sit down.

TerryBill approaches chair tentatively, sits briefly on the edge of it, jumps up and walks up and down while nervously tapping his bottom.

TERRYBILL: *(as one making a stand for truth, head erect)* I can't sit down. *(points to chair and then to his bottom)*

DOCTOR: *(looking up, open-mouthed, with sudden interest)* Why not?

TERRYBILL: I have a touch of sore bottom.

Card is carried across front stage from right.
It reads on one side:

"DOCTOR, I SUFFER FROM SORE BOTTOM."

DOCTOR: *(jumping up in fury, flailing his arms wide)* <u>I'll</u> tell <u>you</u> what you suffer from. *(points vigorously at TerryBill and then at the chair)* I'm the doctor. I do the diagnosis. *(points at himself)*

Card is turned around and reads on the other side:

"I'M THE DOCTOR, HOW DARE YOU
DIAGNOSE YOUR OWN ILLNESS!
I'LL TELL YOU."

Card is carried off left.

TerryBill tries to sit down again but jumps up in pain. Doctor Roarer rises, observes TerryBill closely like a strange animal, rubs his beard, cocks his head, rubs beard and scratches his head. Pauses, thinks, has an idea. Points to couch. TerryBill nods three times, leaves down his hat and stick and lies down on the couch on his back.

The Doctor stabs him in several places with his stethoscope, motions him to turn over on his stomach. After more stabbing and listening around TerryBill's back and waist, he pokes the stethoscope into TerryBill's bottom, e.g., hip or lower spine. TerryBill jumps in agony and begins dancing around holding his bottom.

The Doctor plucks his beard several times, walks up and down shaking his head, dashes over to his desk, consults a large volume, ruminates, walks up and down and then suddenly stabs the air with his right hand, sits down at his desk and begins to write. Stands up and holds a prescription in his hand and points at the still writhing TerryBill.

DOCTOR: Ah, I perceive that you have sore bottom. Do not *(holds up his hand in a negative gesture)* sit for a week and take this medicine. That will be $50.

He holds up five fingers of his left hand and an "0" from thumb and forefinger of his right hand.

The card carriers enter left, walk across the front stage with a card that reads:

"YOU HAVE SORE BOTTOM -
DO NOT SIT - TAKE THIS MEDICINE."

TerryBill stops writhing and twisting. He is furious. He picks up his hat, places it vigorously on his head, picks up his stick and hangs it on his other arm. He takes the prescription from the Doctor and tears it up in shreds and stamps on it.

The card is turned over to read:

"I KNOW I HAVE SORE BOTTOM.
I TOLD YOU SO. YOU PHONY!"

Card is carried off right.

TerryBill stamps out as the Doctor whips out his wallet (or purse) and points at it, pulls the lining out of his pockets, points accusingly at TerryBill. Then as TerryBill turns around and wickedly waves his stick at him, the Doctor shakes his fist at TerryBill.

Doctor pauses, hesitates, looks disgusted, then suddenly begins to laugh. He thumps one hand against another, doubles over, points in ridicule at TerryBill's retreating figure. Then he laughs (silently) again and again. Thumps his desk (if the desk is painted scenery, he thumps the air in front of it).

DOCTOR: *(screaming silently)* Sore bottom could last for weeks, even months, ha, ha, ha.

As the Doctor glowers and fumes and laughs

Card carriers enter right with a card that reads:

"HA, HA, SORE BOTTOM CAN LAST FOR WEEKS AND WEEKS. THE JOKE'S ON YOU."

TerryBill leaves, left-stage, still shaking his stick.

DOCTOR: *(recovering slightly and pointing and beckoning to off stage right)* Next please.

Enter from right, the Youthful Lady Elegant, *dressed in foot-length white gown* *with a black thin belt and black flower on her shoulder. She wears a wide summer hat with a fine veil back and sides and a black band. She carries a long white parasol with a black handle. She hurries into the office, clearing her throat and putting her free hand to her mouth occasionally. She also taps her throat from time to time in a very delicate, ladylike genteel way. Lady mime:*

DRINK YOUR TEA

Sung: Jolly

d d d d l_1 - d
Don't get scared or skittish

f f f r - f
Fight to the finish

d d d d r - d
Be proud to be British

d l_1 s_1
Drink your tea.

d d d d l_1 - d
No matter how you suffer

f f f f r - f
Keep a true stiff upper

f f f f m - m
Eat a good fish supper

f s f
Drink your tea.

VERSE 1
Don't get scared or skittish
Fight to the finish
Be proud to be British
Drink your tea
No matter how you suffer
Keep a true stiff upper
Eat a good <u>fish supper</u>
Drink your tea.

The Doctor is so obsessed with the non-paying TerryBill that he is almost oblivious of the lady patient and treats her in a very perfunctory and absent-minded way. He points her to the couch, motions her to lie down and then to turn over on her stomach, which she does in a completely mystified manner, as the Doctor still rants and raves at the now absent TerryBill.

DOCTOR: *(shaking his fist and pointing after the now absent TerryBill)* I'd like to get you down here and stick a nice long poker *(he holds up a long, stiff index finger)* right into where it hurts the most. O, yes, this stethoscope (ha, ha) right into your 'sore bottom' only harder than before, ha, ha, ha.

Still looking at absent TerryBill, he holds up his left hand and makes a circle with his thumb and forefinger, then holds up and jabs his right index finger into the hole, all the while glowering and shaking his fist to off stage left. Then he lifts up his stethoscope and jams it down into Lady Elegant's bottom, quite forgetting that she is not TerryBill, his non-paying patient.

Lady Elegant jumps up and screams. Doctor is open-mouthed and throws wide his hands in horror. Again she screams and slaps the Doctor's face and begins to beat him about the head and shoulders with her parasol. Doctor puts his hands together in an attitude of prayerful pleading. He retreats, horrified. He is stunned, startled and realizing his mistake, crawls to his chair, covers his head with his arms.

LADY: *(stamping her left foot)* How dare you. I only have a slight summer cold. You fiend. I've heard about men like you. You molester of ladies.

Enter right, card carriers who hold up a card saying:

"HOW DARE YOU? I ONLY HAD A SLIGHT SUMMER COLD. YOU BRUTE, YOU MOLESTER."

Lady continues to beat about Doctor with her umbrella. She stands back, points her finger at Doctor and then ***strides off stage left****, head held high in disdain. Doctor skulks in his corner, looking scared and stunned.*

Curtain

ACT TWO - REJECTION

SCENE ONE: DEMON RUM

The general picture of the stage is that of a seaside strand - promenade (a) to the right - an outdoor cafe, (b) back - the seaside strand and beach and (c) left - the sea wall and promenade.

Right back - a cafe in the same seaside town. A long silver-topped bar runs the half-length right of the stage (painted on the right side screen or an actual prop). If painted, the bartender stands at the end of the bar wiping dishes and miming the act of sending glasses gliding along the bar. If a real bar is used, he stands behind it. There is a striped summer awning over the bar which is located on the strand and is surrounded by chairs, tables and stools.

The rest of the backdrop area and from back left and to front left is all strand promenade with a low stone wall, the sea and boats and beach scenes with boats in the background. Here the ladies or gentlemen are seen to promenade and sit and talk. Here there are also larger tables, chairs and deck-chairs.

The back or screen 'wall' should consist of screen(s) painted to show concession booths, street vendors and horse-drawn traffic of the seaside area, just to the left of, and near the bar. There may be sun umbrellas sprouting from some tables. Some bushes and greenery.

If extras are available, they should come and go jumpily and seem to talk politely and sit in these areas throughout the scene. If extras are NOT available, figures or mannequins can be used with more discrete, less direct lighting. In this case, the areas of less lighting will represent the shade of trees or buildings and the sun will shine only on the cafe, on the sea and on the areas where there are no painted or mannequin figures.

Extras should engage in quick motion, strolling, bowing, raising hats, shaking heads, pointing to scenic spots, shading their eyes to see the sea, sitting, conversing eagerly, ladies curtseying and men bowing as well as similar gentle pursuits. All will be dressed in similar black and white garb to that of TerryBill and Lady Elegant, although such dress may accommodate many different shapes, sizes, ages and hairstyles.

Small boys will be dressed in sailor suits and small girls in pantaloons, blouses, hats and socks. Adult accessories include handbags, purses, watches, waist-high-held box cameras, chains, jewelry, parasols, walking sticks. Children's accessories include soft toys, hoops, hoop-sticks, skipping ropes, kaleidoscopes, and bouncing balls, all of which should, of course, be used in quick motion, as the scene progresses.

Along the front of the cafe should be three or more tall stools with shiny hard tops - plastic, metal or wood, no cushions in sight. The back of the cafe is covered with shelves containing bottles and glasses and an ornate floral design mirror. The bartender is on duty as the scene opens as are some of the extras.

***Enter TerryBill from left**, disconsolate, hobbling along. Seeing the cafe, he brightens and approaches the bar, waving his left hand to summon* *up urgent service. After one brief attempt to sit on a stool, he recoils from the stool, pushes it away and stands for the rest of the scene. He waves his hand again at the bartender, who nods and salutes TerryBill, caps his hand over his right ear to hear TerryBill's order and sets up a glass.*

If only a side screen is used with no physical bar, then a mime can still be effective for setting up glasses or accepting and drinking them.

TERRYBILL: *(setting coins on the bar)* Set 'em up. Set 'em up. Anything to kill the pain.

A card is carried on right to left, reading:

"ANYTHING TO KILL THE PAIN."

He beckons the bartender to set up another, drinks and knocks it back with an obvious effort - a backward jerk of the head, followed by a dreadful shudder, shaking and then a blurb after each drink. He hangs his cane delicately on the stool next to him.

A respectably dressed gentleman, also in white and black suit, tie, socks and shoes sits down on one of the stools, orders a drink, raises his hat to TerryBill, lifts a glass to him in friendly converse, motions to TerryBill to sit on the stool next to him. When TerryBill politely refuses, the stranger takes umbrage, purses his lips and raises his eyebrows to imply that TerryBill is too snobbish.

STRANGER: Oh, so my company isn't good enough, eh?

Stranger drinks up and leaves in disgust, left. TerryBill orders another drink with similar shudders and tremors. He steadies himself against the bar.

BARTENDER: *(holding up three fingers and then jerking an invisible cup three times to his mouth)* You've only had three drinks. You can't be drunk already.

Bartender peers suspiciously at TerryBill.

TERRYBILL: *(shaking his head, motioning negatively with his left hand)* No I'm not drunk. *(points to his legs and moves them with evident pain and strain)* I'm so tired. *(holding out his right hand pitifully as one begging for money and then pointing to his legs)* I am so tired on my feet.

Sore Bottom
The reverse of the previous card
is carried back, left to right, reading:

"I'M SO TIRED STANDING ON MY FEET."

Bartender points to one of the stools, puzzled and frowning.

BARTENDER: In that case sit down. *(gestures generously with open palms towards the stools)* That's why we provide seats - for the poor soul who is tired after his day's work and who wishes to sit and sip a refreshing drink. *(he smiles professionally as one who is pleased with his offered services)*

TerryBill leans heavily on the bar with his forearms, shakes his head in pain and holds up his left hand in a gesture of lifting a drink. Bartender serves him but still with a peer or scrutiny or two of lingering suspicion. TerryBill pays for and knocks back the drink. TerryBill seems a little revived, flexes his back and shakes his legs, takes down his walking stick and walks about a little.

At the same time, two young ladies in long white dresses and black hats sit down at one of the tables and begin to converse. They nod and smile to each other and then smile and nod to TerryBill. TerryBill bows and raises his hat politely. The ladies smile and nod again and giggle behind their hands. They are evidently favorably impressed with TerryBill, who approaches them, bowing and raising his hat again with smiles all around. They point giggling to the vacant seat between them, inviting TerryBill to join them.

TerryBill stands between them ignoring their invitation to sit down but pleased and bashful. He holds his hat modestly across his lower chest and turns away three or four times in bashfulness. Turning back to face the young ladies, he bows, replaces his hat and cheerfully leaning on his walking stick, he begins to smile, converse with the ladies.

TERRYBILL: *(pointing to the general surroundings)* Isn't this such a pleasant resort, ladies, so full of bustle and life and fun.

The ladies smile and giggle and point again more distinctly to the spare chair beside them.

1ST LADY: Do please be seated.

2ND LADY: Yes, we would be honored if you would join us.

During this scene, the bartender is peering at TerryBill and the ladies suspiciously, leaning over the counter and leaning forward to squint at them, then leaning backwards to get them in better focus - his whole demeanor bespeaking distrust, suspicion, wariness. At times he puts his hand behind his ear, as he leans forward to hear what is being said. Eventually, he leans forward and points a vicious finger at the group.

BARTENDER: No idle pickups here. Are you ladies going to order a meal or not. *(he wipes the counter, disconsolately)*

TERRYBILL: *(to ladies, pointing to the bar)* Can I treat you?

He mimes a drink to each of the ladies who nod with enthusiasm. Bartender beams with enthusiasm. TerryBill orders three drinks, holding up three fingers and lifting an invisible drink. TerryBill approaches the bar, digs deeply into his trouser pocket, looks around at the girls in embarrassment at his lack of funds but, after a few tries, finally places enough on the bar counter to satisfy the bartender who beams again and hands over three drinks, two of which TerryBill takes over to the ladies and one of which he raises in a toast to them. They all drink and smile and nod at each other.

The ladies again point to the vacant chair but TerryBill declines regretfully. Taking his refusal as an end to the meeting the two young ladies rise, curtsey and shake hands with TerryBill politely.

1ST LADY: Thank you so much.

2ND LADY: What a pity you can't join us.

A card is carried on stage from right to left, reading:

"THANKS FOR THE DRINKS –
PITY YOU CANNOT JOIN US"

The ladies mime ***FISH AND CHIPS*** *and collect two wrapped-up packets.*

FISH AND CHIPS

Sung: Fast

VERSE 1 AND REFRAIN:
s d - d m s d^1 t
O I'll have some fish and chips please
d^1 r^1 l - l - l - l
If that's all right with you
f r - r - r f t - t - t
Not too much grease - some mushy peas
l s s s - f m
And salt and vinegar too
s d - d m - s d^1 - d^1 t
No more the dainty dinner do
d^1 r^1 l - l - l - l
No more them dunking dips
l s s - s s - t t l
I say if it's all right with you
s - s s f r d
I'll have some fish and chips

VERSE 1 AND REFRAIN:
O I'll have some fish and chips please
If that's all right with you
Not too much grease - some mushy peas
And salt and vinegar too
No more the dainty dinner do
No more them dunking dips
I say if it's all right with you
I'll have some fish and chips

VERSE 2:
Now the Admiral was in the pink
His ships were spiffy clean
Your Majesty what do you think?
He asks the blooming Queen
Says the Queen I absolutely love
This fleet of men and ships
The only thing they need more of
Is good old fish and chips

VERSE 3:
Well my Uncle Ray drops dead one day
We lay him down in flowers
Then we start a party right away
To brighten those sad hours
Ahh . . . suddenly he bolts upright
And fear and terror grips . . .
We ask, What brought you back? He cried
I smell some fish and chips

VERSE 4:
See I knew a handsome man I say
As cheerful as the moon
Says he Come visit me some day -
So I showed up right soon
He asked What would you like to do?
We've some nice river trips
I say if it's all right with you
We'll have some fish and chips

As the ladies leave, waving a pretty and ladylike goodbye, TerryBill looks embarrassed, beckons them back, changes his mind and signals that he himself might join them, pointing to himself and then to the ladies and the promenade, but the ladies do not grasp his point and walk off together conversing cheerfully. ***The narration card is then carried off stage left.***

TerryBill disconsolately walks up and down, leans his elbows on the bar counter, shaking his head, holding his head in his hands and ruminating sadly.

TERRYBILL: *(signaling a drink and counting at his money, he peers at his money, searches for more, signals 'just a wee' one by holding his left index finger and thumb closely together to the bartender who peers suspiciously at TerryBill, drawing back and forward and squinting as before)*

BARTENDER: What's the matter?

TERRYBILL: *(pointing to his legs)* I can't stand anymore, my legs are killing me. (*He bends forward in pain and buckles his knees and points to his legs in agony. The bartender points vigorously out to the strand - left stage.)*

Card is carried out left to right as follows:

"KEEP YOUR LAST PENNIES IF YOU CAN'T STAND UP. I CAN'T GIVE YOU ANOTHER DRINK ANYWAY."

Card is held in place as TerryBill hobbles off along the strand, left stage, leaning on his stick and wincing at times. ***He leaves stage left****, in some misery of soul as well as physical discomfort and mimes:*

FOOD AIN'T AS GOOD

Sung: Slow

VERSE 1:

t_1 - r m m m - m r m s s s - l
I ain't shed no tears over onions in years
s - l t l s m r t_1 r
It seems that good smells have been banned
t_1 - r m m m - m r m s s s l
My taste bud's a dud when I eat a new spud
s - l t l s - m m m - m
And the eggs are so weak they can't stand
t r^1 t t - t l - s l l - l l
The dog that I had went a stark staring mad
s - l t l s - m r t_1 r
When it smelt a fresh steak from the store
t_1 - r m m m - m r - m s s s - l
Now the meat has no smell and the dog sleeps so well
s - l t l s - m m m - m
Oh the food ain't as good as before

Sore Bottom

VERSE 1:
I ain't shed no tears over onions in years
It seems that good smells have been banned
My taste bud's a dud when I eat a new spud
And the eggs are so weak they can't stand
The dog that I had went a stark staring mad
When it smelt a fresh steak from the store
Now the meat has no smell and the dog sleeps so well
Oh the food ain't as good as before
No the food ain't as good as before.

VERSE 2:
The tomatoey smell was so strong I could tell
It had grown up on all loving care
And the scarred ugly fruit was so sweet and so cute
I was eager as a bee for my share
So let's get the good oldtime taste back in food
Must we wait for a pie in the sky?
Tell me, O tell, where is sharp taste and smell?
Where's the catfish that made the cat cry? *(sniff, sniff)*

REFRAIN: *(Tune: Repeat last 4 lines of verse)*
I'm a-looking for good and plain old fashioned food
With a crunch or a munch I declare
With a smell and a smack and a tang and a crack
I'm as keen as a bee for my share

<u>Curtain</u>

ACT TWO - REJECTION

SCENE TWO:

UNCLE'S FACTORY

The office of Uncle Makem Sohrbottom, president of the Makem Sohrbottom Furniture Co. The main items of furniture are a desk cluttered with phones, two office chairs, one behind and one in front of the desk, right back nearby. Nearby a couch or sofa (the same items as in Scene One). Other furniture which may be real or painted on screens include such items as water cooler, lamps, pictures, busts, vase of flowers, filing cabinets, small set of shelves, coffee tables and the like. The floor is covered with rugs or carpet.

The general impression is of a prosperous executive's early 20th century office. The long wall of the office will be the backdrop area (whether there is in use actual backdrops or screens or frames covered in painted cardboard/paper)

The backdrop area, as opposed to the left and right stage "walls" or side screens should not contain many of the items of furnishings listed above, but should be mainly clear, except perhaps for a vase of flowers or similar small items, or a pictorial description of the company.

Across 70% of the backdrop area, about 7 or 8 feet above the floor is a banner headline reading

"The Makem Sohrbottom Furniture Co at Work" and ranged across this backdrop area are six large pictures of workers typifying the company's activities. These exhibits are for the benefit of explaining the work and success of the company to visitors, such as buyers, suppliers, potential investors, possible executives.

They consist of the following, ranging from right to left.

1. JOINERS

Picture of a carpenter.

2. MAINTENANCE

Picture of a cleaner, painter or repairer.

3. DRIVERS

Picture of a horse drover.

Below these there is a running headline MANUAL WORKERS. These jobs may be represented by symbols such as

(1) saw and hammer for carpenter

(2) spanner, brush/mop for maintenance and

(3) horse and cart for driver - delivery.

4. BUYER

Picture of a buyer, well dressed, sitting at a desk, studying wood and blueprints.

5. SALESMAN

Picture of a besuited salesman sitting on the outer side of a desk in front of a wholesale manager.

6. MANAGER

Picture of a manager, behind his desk, answering a phone-call on an early 20th century phone.

Below these 3 pictures is a running headline WHITECOLLAR WORKERS.

Again, if preferred, these three occupations may be represented by symbols such as:

(4) unfinished wood, designs and plans for buyer

(5) money, currency bills, cash, grabbing hands for salesmen.

(6) phone, a pointing hand, pen and ink for manager.

As the curtain rises, Uncle Makem, a large bearded man, in black suit with white accessories, is sitting behind his desk, back right, shuffling papers, answering one of the phones, leaning back and closing his eyes for inspiration, then opening his eyes, screaming "I got it", jabbing the air with his right index finger and then scribbling furiously on a piece of paper.

A card is carried in, saying:

"UNCLE MAKEM SOHRBOTTOM,
BIG TIME CREATOR OF JOBS."

***Enter TerryBill**, as before, tentatively, still tired and touching his rear end tenderly at times. He is greeted with uproarious enthusiasm by his uncle, who pumps his arm in a vigorous handshake.*

UNCLE: *(throwing wide his arms)* What brings you here to my place of work? *(he points to the pictures)*

TERRYBILL: Work *(he mimes sawing, cutting and nailing and pulls the lining out of both pants' pockets)*

Card is carried on right to left, reading:

"I'M BROKE UNCLE, I NEED A JOB"

Uncle Makem jumps for joy.

UNCLE: Great! I need good men to steer my firm. *(He points to the white collar section on the wall and simulates a sailor steering a ship. He is so pleased he jumps again and thumps TerryBill on the back)* But you're broke and you need a job, right?

TerryBill nods and the same card as on the last occasion is carried back left to right, reading as before.

"I'M BROKE UNCLE, I NEED A JOB!"

Uncle Makem takes TerryBill by the hand and leads him towards the 'White Collar Section' of the pictures on the wall. He points to it proudly and squares his chest, pointing to himself and to TerryBill, then pointing to his head and to TerryBill's head.

UNCLE: Brain workers, white collar workers, that's what we need. *(points to manual workers, dismissively)* Anyone can work with their hands *(he simulates hammering, sweeping, driving a horse, sawing)* but it takes a good man *(puts his thumbs up and points to TerryBill and himself)* to do brainwork. *(points to his head).*

Once again, proudly, he points to the white collar workers then to TerryBill.

UNCLE: These poor beggars have to stand all day *(he points to the manual workers)* but these *(he points to white collar workers and then to a* *chair)* get to sit at their work. *(he beams on TerryBill)*

A card is carried in, reading:

"YOU CAN HAVE ANY GOOD, SIT DOWN, WHITE COLLAR JOB IN MY FIRM."

Uncle Makem opens his arms to welcome TerryBill to the firm.

The card is flipped over, reading:

"WELCOME TO THE FAMILY BUSINESS. YOUR DAYS OF SOWING WILD OATS ARE OVER."

TerryBill winces, touches his bottom tenderly and points his stick at the Manual Jobs.

TERRYBILL: I don't mind standing all day *(he simulates hard work, cutting, sawing and so on. He smiles at the idea)* It's starting at the bottom *(he holds out his right hand low down at knee level, then raises it)* and working my way to the top. *(Uncle Makem shakes his head and moves his hands across each other in a scissors fashion, rejecting the idea. He points to his chest proudly)*

UNCLE: I'm a plain spoken, honest man. Nephew works his way up in firm is pure hypocrisy. *(shakes his head)* I won't bear it.

Card is carried on, reading:

"I WILL NEVER HAVE A NEPHEW OF MINE DOING MANUAL LABOR, STANDING ON HIS FEET ALL DAY."

The card is flipped over, reading:

"WE SOHRBOTTOMS ARE BRAIN WORKERS. ALL BEST JOBS ARE SITTING DOWN USING BRAINS LAD."

TerryBill looks tearful, puts his hands together in a prayerful pleading gesture and points to the pictures of manual workers.

TERRYBILL: Please give me one of those jobs.

UNCLE: *(pointing to the white collar section and smiling kindly)* But my boy you can have one of these good jobs – you're my nephew. *(he taps his chest, TerryBill shakes his head and points again to the manual jobs.)*

TERRYBILL: *(pathetically)* Could I not have one of these jobs? *(he mimes hammering, sawing,* *cleaning, wrenching a spanner - smiles brightly)* I like hard work.

UNCLE: *(frowning and getting annoyed)* Certainly not! *(he points to the manual work pictures and cuts his hand vigorously across and away from his chest)* Absolutely not! *(shaking his head)*

A card is carried in and out, reading:

"THE FAMILY GAVE YOU A GOOD EDUCATION. YOU'RE A BRAIN WORKER. YOU CAN SIT AT YOUR WORK – NOT STAND ALL DAY."

TerryBill shakes his head sadly in rejecting his Uncle's offer. Uncle becomes at first quite upset, then irate. Uncle points accusingly at TerryBill.

A card is carried in, reading:

"SO YOU WILL NOT ACCEPT RESPONSIBILITY! YOU WANT AN EASY, SIMPLE LIFE - NEVER."

The card is turned over as Uncle waits expectantly. It reads:

"LOOK UP. USE YOUR EDUCATION. BE PROUD TO BE A SOHRBOTTOM – TAKE A GOOD SIT-DOWN JOB."

TerryBill sighs, touches his rear tenderly, turns away.

TERRYBILL: No. I can't do that, Uncle. I wish I could.

Uncle is furious, points to the door.

UNCLE: Get out, you lout. You drunken bum. Never darken my three pile carpet *(he points to the floor)* ever again.

TerryBill humbly and regretfully limps out, turns around with one last pathetic gesture turning his pockets wide out but Uncle is unmoved and points to the door.

TerryBill sniffs and sobs and hobbles out miserably as a card is carried in and out, reading:

"YOU DRUNKEN LAYABOUT BE GONE!"

TerryBill leaves left, Uncle remains on stage pointing to door.

<u>Curtain</u>

ACT THREE - A FORTUNATE MEETING

SCENE ONE:

STANDING OVATION

Overview: *The scene is a modification of Act Two, Scene One, i.e., a different part of the strand-promenade. The cafe is gone and in its place is a bandstand area and park.*

Scene opens on a long and broad, overall view of the seafront strand or promenade, left a pedestrian way beside the wall that separates beach from the seaside town. The right side screen now represents a park which is filled with (a selection from) strolling holidaymakers, deck chairs, flower beds, benches, small covered bandstands, small concession booths selling seafood or candy or souvenirs. Bicycle ice cream sellers and other street-hawkers may also be seen.

Next to the park there is a driving area for tramcars, horse drawn jaunting cars headed up by a driver and dog mascot. Here and there are spillover pedestrians. Some obnoxious and horseless riding-machines may also occasionally invade this formerly happy street.

The center and left and backdrop is a modification of Act Two - Scene One. However, the bar is gone. The stools and tables are also gone per se, although these may be redeployed in order to contribute to the general scene which is, briefly, a panoramic view of the strand and includes beach, sun bathers, distant hills, clouds, sea and boats - all, of course, early 20th century in style.

Around left center stage near the road is a moderately extensive meeting area consisting of a bandstand or similar platform, round or square, with chairs in front of it. Soon a religious meeting will be held here. Extras or mannequins should be used as in the Act Two - Scene One stage instructions, either as attending the meeting or as occasional spectators or passersby.

None of the props at the meeting should indicate any particular religion or denomination. (e.g., no crosses, crescents, angels, etc.) As the curtain rises there are a few extras or mannequins on stage.

***Enter from right the members of a religious meeting** who take up their places in the bandstand and at the surrounding seats but remain standing for a hymn. They are all dressed in white hats, suits and dresses but with black accessories - umbrellas, handbags or purse belts, shoes, socks, walking sticks, watches, pearls, large black books.*

First onto the platform is a fat man playing a big bass drum hung on his chest (drummer). Second onto the platform is a small skinny woman playing an accordion (accordionist). Third onto the platform is a tall skinny man playing a trumpet (trumpeter). Fourth onto the platform is a fat woman playing a trombone (trombonist). Fifth onto the platform, taking his prime place middle front of the platform, is a full bearded preacher holding a large black book (preacher).

First to sit among the audience is a tall thin male witness (Man Witness). Second to sit in audience is a small fat female witness (Woman Witness). Third to sit in the audience is a young pretty female singer awaiting her cue. (This is Mavis the Girl Singer).

The group immediately strike up a hymn, still standing, left center of stage, near the promenade. If accompanying music is being played on the piano, an appropriate tune at this point would be "Whiter than the Snow." They sing with great fervor and much hand clapping, conducted and led by Preacher.

After a few lines of song, a great spray of black mud splashes over them, soiling their white clothes. They shake their fists at the offstage motorist.

A card is carried on and off stage right to left center, reading:

"SPLASH - NO LONGER WHITER THAN SNOW THANKS TO THE MAD MOTORIST."

A card is carried on left to right, reading:

"WATCH WHERE YOU'RE STANDING IN FUTURE" *yells the motorist.*

and is turned over to read:

"WHY? ARE YOU COMING BACK?" *replies the preacher..*

The card is carried off right.

The meeting group shake themselves down and brush off some of the mud from their clothes. The Preacher is livid and begins to rant and rave wildly, hitting his big black book, shaking his fist at the now departed motorist, pointing to the sky and then to the ground, then at the motorist, tearing at his hair and so on.

***A card is carried on stage from right** while the preacher's diatribe continues. This rather longer than average speech can be read aloud* *by a member of the audience if some of the audience are unable to read it. But otherwise it should be held for a minute or so, instead of the usual few seconds.*

It reads as follows:

"THE RIDING MACHINES ARE A MENACE TO BOTH MAN AND HORSE AND SHOULD NEVER BE PERMITTED TO CAREER AROUND OTHERWISE CIVILIZED HAUNTS WITHOUT EVEN A RED FLAG OF WARNING. THESE VILE CONTRAPTIONS, IN A MORE ENLIGHTENED FUTURE, WILL NO DOUBT BE BANNED TO THE REMOTER REGIONS. HOW CAN THEY BE ALLOWED TO REMAIN AS A MENACE TO POLITE SOCIETY?"

The card is carried off stage left.

The other members of Preacher's group placate him, smiling and pointing upwards, and Preacher eventually is subdued and calls for another hymn. Band plays and all join in another (silent) hymn, holding up their black books.

Enter TerryBill*, tired and leaning on his stick, hobbling a little and wincing as he touches his rear end occasionally. Seeing the* *group standing singing a hymn, he brightens and joins them, hooking his cane on his arms, he stands beside Man Witness who offers to share a hymn book or sheet with him. He joins in the vigorous singing. At the end of the hymn, the Preacher motions to all to sit down. All sit except TerryBill.*

Preacher begins to declaim from his black book, pointing to the sky and to the earth and hitting the book frequently. Raising his right fist, he shakes it in the sky, while waving the black book at his audience. Suddenly, Preacher sees that TerryBill is still standing and motions him to sit, then continues with his speech. He does not at first notice that TerryBill is still standing.

Woman Witness politely signals TerryBill to sit down, but he continues to stand. Mavis motions TerryBill vigorously to sit down but TerryBill looks miserable, his knees buckle and he kneels on the stage, burying his face in the seat of a chair and sobbing.

Sore Bottom
A card is carried on from left to right, it reads:

"I CANNOT STAND UP ANY LONGER"

TerryBill begins to thump the seat of the chair in pain and distress. The Preacher stops. Mavis jumps up and waves to the Preacher.

MAVIS: *(pointing to TerryBill)* This young man is under conviction from your preaching. *(points to Preacher)* He *(points to TerryBill)* says he cannot stand up any longer.

Mavis points to her legs and shakes them stiffly. Preacher clutches his black book to his chest and raises the other hand in a salute to the skies. He descends the platform and approaches TerryBill, still preaching, striking his left hand and his heart with the black book, pointing to TerryBill, to the sky, and to the earth. The rest of the group follow Preacher and form a ring around the back, right and left of TerryBill, who can still be seen clearly by the audience as he kneels and sobs in great agony on the seat of the chair.

A card is carried on and of from right to left, reading:

"LIFE CAN BE PAINFUL."

Preacher places his hand on TerryBill's shoulder and the others help TerryBill to stand up. They shake hands with him, introduce him to each other and to Mavis. TerryBill raises his hat to
Mavis, who shyly turns away. All shake hands with TerryBill and pat him on back.

TerryBill mimes THE SWALLOW SONG

Sung: Rollicking

VERSE 1:

m m m - m m m - m
I'd like to be a swallow
m r - d d r - d
A-flying high and low
m s - s l s - s m - m
He zips away like a flying machine
f s - s f m - r
To where he wants to go
m f s - s l - s - s s - m
Now, if such a flittery critter
m - f s - s m d - r
Can zip and dip and soar
d - r m - m s_1 - s_1 l_1 d - d
Then we could fly to the hills up high
m r d - d d - d
And find a golden door

REFRAIN:

```
d   r   m - m - m   m - m - m   m - m
O the  zippery, flippery swallow
 m - m    r - d     d    d - d
Goes a swinging in the dawn
   m        s - s   l - s - s    s - m
Through bushes into the hollow
    f - f     s - s - s     f - m - m   r
While the snoozy birds still yawn
 m  f    s - s - s - l    s - s - s - m
He's a flyer that nothing can follow
 m     s     s     m    d    r
He's there and then he's gone
 d   r   m - m - m   m - m - m   m - m
For  the   jittery,   flittery   swallow
   m    m   r - d - d    d - d - d   d
Goes a  looping and swooping on
```

VERSE 2:
O the swallow has a passport
That always gets him by
I wish I had the secret zip
That makes his engines fly
Though the woods are hung with greenery
And bushes thick and high
He's up and down and all around
In the flick of a winking eye

TERRYBILL: *(stretching out a leg)* I could not stand up any longer.

PREACHER: *(pointing to the sky and waving his black book)* Of course not - we all need heavenly strength . . .

The group reform, band and preacher to the platform, others to stand and sing another hymn. This time TerryBill and Mavis share a hymn book and smile at each other occasionally.

Briefly the two witnesses stand up in turn and give their testimony, pointing down low and then up high and throwing their arms in the air and shouting Hallelujah to the nods, smiles and approval of the others.

The group should be arranged so that TerryBill and Mavis are the central figures. TerryBill and Mavis receive encouraging nods of approval and smiles from the rest of the group including Preacher.

A card is carried in from left to right, reading:

"LOVE AT FIRST SIGHT - AN ENGAGEMENT."

It is carried out right.

After the hymn, the meeting breaks up into small groups who chat together. The Preacher declaims and waves his black book to the witnesses. The band begin to practice together and TerryBill and Mavis join hands and stroll to the left stage nearer the seaside where they join other promenaders. They approach left front stage and Mavis points out to sea. TerryBill, touching the small of his back, which is aching, leans gratefully on the sea wall.

MAVIS: See those clouds. *(she shivers)* It's getting cold!

TerryBill places his hand protectively across her shoulders.

A card is carried on from right to left, reading:

"BUT TERRYBILL, DARK CLOUDS ARE BREWING ON THE HORIZON"

The card is flipped over to read on the reverse side.

"AH, THE COURSE OF TRUE LOVE."

***This card is carried over in front of where Mavis and TerryBill are standing,** looking over the sea. Mavis shivering and TerryBill reassuring. Both are shading their eyes with their hands and pointing out to sea.*

The card is then carried off left as the stage lights blink two or three times. If there is piano accompaniment there is a roll of thunder on the piano. With lights flickering, all run left and then right backwards, as though the film projector had reversed the scene, inadvertently. This reversal is repeated once.

When lights come on fully, they are much lower. All umbrellas are raised as all scatter and run back and forth. TerryBill takes shelter with Mavis. Ranting and raving, the Preacher hits his book and shakes his fist at the storm.

The group takes shelter with each other. Rain begins to fall. All begin to move to left and right and back, scurrying for shelter in the bandstand and under trees or under umbrellas.

Curtain

ACT THREE - A FORTUNATE MEETING
SCENE TWO:
BUT FATHER IS A HARD MAN

The scene is set in the front yard of the home farm of Mavis. On the backdrop is a small farmhouse with porch, surrounded by rough overgrown hedges, and further back, hills and ploughed acres and green fields and cows. Sidedrops show the same farm land in the distance with hedges separating the stageground from the painted background.

At the corner of left stage back just beside the hedge and protruding across the backdrop is a small carriage with seats for two, a hood folded down and two large wheels. The horse that pulls it cannot be seen, as they are hidden by the hedge but it should be possible to pull the carriage some way to the left so that it either rolls off stage or out of right behind the hedge. Whether the carriage is real or simulated, (e.g., built of wood or plastic) it should be strong enough and mobile enough to hold one passenger in the seat as it rolls out of right.

Right stage, at the corner of back and right, there is a hay cart lying still filled with hay. This cart should be large enough for a person to lie on it. However, it need not be mobile.

Center stage is an open space, a slightly raised platform for parties, barbecues or tea parties. This should consist of two or three steps and cover enough of center stage to hold seven or eight people standing close together or three or four people in conversation, spread out.

The rest of the stage should be scattered with the occasional farm implements or equipment. For example, a few of the following, a milking stool, a bucket, a hoe, an old abandoned plough, a lost cart wheel, a water pump, a rake, a spade. The number of such will depend on the size of the stage, but the whole stage will be covered in grass with a few crosswalks of paved stone - except, of course, for the slightly raised center stage party area, the real-life purpose of which is to avoid having guests standing on mud.

As the scene opens, the guests (at the invitation of Mavis) begin to enter.

A card is carried on and off from left to right, reading:

"A WEDDING REHEARSAL."

Enter the Preacher, a Trumpeter, a Trombonist, a Drummer, an Accordionist, Man Witness and Woman Witness *followed by Mavis herself holding hands with*

TerryBill. They arrange themselves for a wedding rehearsal with the preacher holding his black book in front of him. Mavis and TerryBill standing facing the preacher and hold hands, as the others gather around. After posing in this format for a few seconds, the group breaks up and forms into groups, for example, TerryBill and Mavis conversing cheerfully: Preacher and the witnesses laughing and nodding to each other, the bandpersons forming a group and practicing informally with each other. TerryBill still finds difficulty standing, shows signs of pain at his rear end, hobbles over to the hay cart and lies down in it with considerable relief.

Mavis follows him and stands nearby, clasping her hands, holding up her arms in ecstasy, then folding her arms across her chest, looking pensive. She points to her family farm then to TerryBill and herself, then to the surroundings indicating her bliss at having her home here soon after her marriage. TerryBill, lies back nodding and pointing to the surrounding farm with obvious approval.

Similarly, the wedding rehearsal party nod approvingly at the surroundings and at

TerryBill and Mavis as being an ideal and lucky couple. Everybody is happy.

Enter from right Farmer Workacre, *the father of the bride to be. He is large, fat, bearded and irate. He approaches the wedding rehearsal party with fierce contempt.*

FATHER: *(to Mavis, raising his hands in horror)* What is this?

MAVIS: *(in a pleading gesture, hands turned upwards)* Father, you know you agreed to a wedding rehearsal.

A card is carried in from right, reading:

"FATHER, YOU KNOW YOU AGREED TO A WEDDING REHEARSAL."

FATHER: *(fiercely gesticulating and shooing away the entire party)* Forget it. No wedding - all go home! I'm a plain spoken man.

The card is flipped over to read:

"FORGET THE REHEARSAL – THERE WILL BE NO WEDDING - ALL GO HOME."

Card is carried off left.

Party begins to disperse.

MAVIS: *(beckoning the party to return, naively and innocently)* But father, why - why no wedding. *(pointing to TerryBill)* You know I am engaged to TerryBill. *(she points to TerryBill and to herself and places a ring on her left hand).*

FATHER: Yes, but I'm a plain spoken country man and I say - no wedding.

Mavis begins to sob and weep into her hand, then breaks loose from this mode and cries to the sky, throwing wide her arms.

MAVIS: Why, oh why father?

Guests stand around, in horror and astonishment and fear.

FATHER: *(pointing to TerryBill on the hay wagon)* Look at that layabout. He will not work. I spoke to his uncle. His *(points to TerryBill)* own uncle says he will not work.

Card is carried in from left and off to right, reading:

"TERRYBILL IS A LAYABOUT.
HIS OWN UNCLE SAYS HE WILL NOT WORK!
HOW WILL HE SUPPORT YOU?"

Father jumps up and down in rage and points at TerryBill reclining on the hay cart. He points to the ground and at TerryBill.

FATHER: Get off that hay. *(to Mavis remonstrating and crossing his hands in a negative scissors motion)* This is no good. All our family have been hardworking farmers for generations.

TerryBill gets off the hay cart stiffly and rubs his rear end and hobbles a bit as he stands. The rest of the party look on uneasily as TerryBill, Mavis and father argue.

MAVIS: *(nodding her head and pointing to TerryBill)* Yes, he will work, won't you TerryBill?

TERRYBILL: *(nodding his head)* Certainly.

FATHER: *(pointing to TerryBill with a sly look)* Don't you fool me young man. *(points his thumb at his chest)* I'm a plain spoken, honest man. I'll put you to the test.

TERRYBILL: All right.

MAVIS: *(approving and smiling)* Yes, that's fair isn't it TerryBill?

TerryBill nods cheerfully.

FATHER: *(walking up and down thinking - he brightens)* I know.

A card is carried on from right, reading:

"I KNOW - WORK ON THE FARM HERE. CAN YOU RIDE HORSES OR DRIVE A TRACTOR OR MILK A COW?"

TerryBill touches his bottom tenderly and looks uncomfortable and shakes his head brokenly.

The card is flipped over to read:

"WELL, NO SIR, NOT AT THE MOMENT. MAYBE IN A FEW WEEKS TIME."

Card is carried off to left.

Father is furious. He jumps in the air.

FATHER: In a few weeks time, on the farm, you'll milk a cow *(he mimes milking and sneers)* Oh yes, that's great. *(shaking his arms at the* *whole company to get out)* Get out. Scram. Vamoose.

Mavis begins to sob and is led away towards the house by father. Father turns around and waves a wide arm banishing everyone from the farmyard.

The wedding party slinks out off stage left looking miserable and waving goodbye to Mavis and TerryBill.

TerryBill, also miserable, hobbles off right with the help of his walking stick. He blows a kiss at Mavis but it has the effect only of producing a weak wave and a shower of sobs in response.

TerryBill leaves stage right. Only Mavis and father are left as he guides her weeping to the door of the farm house.

A Reversal Reversed

This last scene is run back and then run forward again. Everyone walks backwards to where they where when Father screamed "Vamoose." The "reel" has reversed again and sticks at the word vamoose for a moment, then, as before, father waves the guests away and the guests retreat off stage.

Sore Bottom

TerryBill blows a kiss and leaves again right as the last scene is repeated in quick motion all much as before.

Lights dim.

Curtain

ACT THREE - A FORTUNATE MEETING

SCENE THREE:
A JOB FOR TERRYBILL

The same farmyard scene, later the same day. A few props should have been rearranged or moved to show passages of time.

***Enter TerryBill** from right, with a pair of shears and begins to merrily clip the hedges of the farmyard. Since this is standing up work, it does not bother him. He merrily sings a bright song, thus alerting father who approaches stealthily, shotgun in hand, from backstage (or his cabin door if operable). Father stalks upon TerryBill as though catching a poacher or intruder. He peers a little shortsightedly at TerryBill, not realizing who he is.*

FATHER: Hands up! You scoundrel.

TerryBill faces Father and throws up both hands, one of which still holds the scissors.

Mavis follows father out into the yard, also from back-stage. She recognizes TerryBill and throws up her hands in horror.

MAVIS: *(pointing to TerryBill and then at her heart)* Oh father, it's only TerryBill. Don't shoot.

Father lowers the shotgun, but still glowers at TerryBill and points off stage right with his left arm stretched out in a get out gesture.

FATHER: TerryBill, eh? I told you to get out.

A card is carried on from right, reading:

"NO DAUGHTER OF MINE WILL MARRY AN UNEMPLOYED LAYABOUT. GET GOING."

TERRYBILL: *(smiling and happy and pointing to his chest and then to the shears)*

Card is flipped over to read:

"BUT I HAVE A JOB - CUTTING HEDGES."

Mavis claps her hands together in joy.

FATHER: That job won't last long. There's only a few hedges to be cut. *(shrugs, belittling the work by waving the back of his hand at it in a deprecating gesture)*

MAVIS: *(sweeping her arms around to indicate the whole farm)* But father, there's plenty of hard work to be done around the farm. TerryBill cannot do all of it but he will do <u>some</u> of it. Won't you TerryBill?

TerryBill nods vigorously and smiles.

A card is carried on from right, reading:

"TERRYBILL SAYS HE CAN
1. FIX THE FENCES,
2. PAINT THE HOUSE,
3. GROOM THE HORSES,
4. PLOUGH WITH A HORSE."

Father contemplates and nods approvingly at TerryBill.

FATHER: Why not?

The card is flipped over to read:

"YOU WANT TO DO THE HARDEST JOBS AROUND THE FARM? THERE'S NO SITTING DOWN ON THESE JOBS, TERRYBILL. IS THAT O.K. WITH YOU?"

TerryBill nods happily and embraces Mavis. Father scratches his head and shakes it in wonder.

FATHER: If it's O.K. with you TerryBill, it's O.K. with me.

TerryBill mimes

WHAT A GOOD DOG.

Sung: Cheerful and Rollicking

VERSE 1:

d r m m m - m r d m s s - s
Now some dogs are so bold they won't do what they're told
l s m d - d r m l_1
But still they expect to get food
d m m m - m r d m s s - s
Why should they get fed and why should they get bed
l - l s m d r m - r d
When their manners are not very good.

Sore Bottom

REFRAIN:
m - m s s s s l t d^1 - d^1 l - d^1
I will sit up and beg and then hold up a leg
l s m d - d r m - l_1 m l_1
I'll stick out my tongue and agree (you'll see)
d m m m m r d m s s s
O please let me do all you're asking me to
l s m d r m r d r d
O what a good dog I will be (you'll see)

VERSE 1:
Now some dogs are so bold they won't do what they're told
But still they expect to get food
Why should they get fed and why should they get bed
When their manners are not very good?

VERSE 2:
I'll go round in a loop or I'll jump through a hoop
I'll crawl on the ground and lie low
I'll cover my face and pretend to say Yes
I'll bring back whatever you throw.

VERSE 3
It is quite an affront if you can't do a stunt
Like cringe away down and play dead
If you can't earn your pay in some groveling way
I don't think you ought to get paid.

VERSE 4
I will sit up and beg and then hold up a leg
I'll stick out my tongue and agree *(you'll see)*
O please let me do all you're asking me to
O what a good dog I will be *(you'll see)*.

Father shakes hands with TerryBill. First father, then TerryBill kiss Mavis in congratulations. Father ushers them both, arm in arm, towards the farmhouse.

TerryBill throws his hat in the air and catches it, then bows to Mavis to allow her to enter the house before him. TerryBill then bows to father, also to give him precedence into the farmhouse. Then bows to the audience, as

Curtain

ACT THREE - A FORTUNATE MEETING
SCENE FOUR:
A SORE BUT HAPPY END

The same. A few props should have been rearranged to show the passage of time. At first the lights show a sunny and cloudless day. A few ribbons have been tied to the hay cart, the carriage, the farmhouse door and perhaps a few of the other props. Except for TerryBill and Mavis, all actors have some rice or confetti in their pockets or purses.

***Enter the band of witnesses**, as before, led by the preacher with his large black book. Some have umbrellas, all have large black books as before. The Drummer, still with his drum, follows the Preacher, then the female accordionist, then the trumpeter, then the female trombonist. All are playing their instruments in a vigorous hymn as they form an ensemble on the picnic/barbecue area center stage, facing the audience. At center is the preacher and right and left of the group are the male and female witness, respectively.*

After a brief pause, TerryBill enters last of all and takes up his place in front of the preacher. He may either be dressed as before or wearing a black suit with white accessories by contrast. TerryBill is waiting to be married to Mavis. His back is turned to the audience for part of this scene and he should remind the audience of the cause of all his adventures from time to time. A slight wincing, tenderly touching his rear end occasionally, a twitch and a touch now and again will be sufficient to remind the audience of the title of the play.

At these preliminary activities, the male and female witnesses take turns to give vigorous testimonies with much black-book waving and hitting. Pointing high up, low down and directly at the audience. This is followed by more vigorous hymn playing and singing with the trombone and trumpet pointing high up and low down to simulate keys, scales and pitches.

After three to five minutes of this preparation and joyful waiting for the bride, Mavis is led out by her father, accompanied by a much slower tune on the off stage piano (if any) - the wedding march. "Here comes by bride," by Wagner. Mavis wears a white bridal gown, white hat and veil and carries flowers, while her father wears a coarse, heavy ill-fitting black suit, white shirt, bowler hat and black boots. Father leaves Mavis beside TerryBill and steps to the right. Mavis is now standing to the left of TerryBill, also with her back to the audience. She turns to TerryBill and smiles as she takes his hand.

Preacher rushes through the wedding ceremony in about 30 seconds and then addresses Mavis.

PREACHER: Do you take this man to be your lawful wedded husband.

Mavis nods.

PREACHER: *(now addressing TerryBill)* Do you take this woman to be your lawful wedded wife.

TerryBill nods.

PREACHER: Then bla, bla, bla, bla - I now pronounce you man and wife.

Preacher closes his book sharply, nods and smiles and bows slightly.

TerryBill places a ring on the finger of Mavis, kisses her and then leads her towards the carriage, back left. The preacher and the male witnesses kiss the bride, others shake hands with the couple and throw confetti or rice on them as they edge towards the carriage.

Suddenly the female witness points to the sky and everyone scurries around seeking shelter and opening umbrellas. Accordionist gives her umbrella to Mavis. The lights black out and come on again three times. A bright flash of lightning blazes up the scene and rain begins to fall.

The preacher begins to jump up and down in fury, hits his book and then shakes it at the heavens in anger. He shakes his other fist at the skies several times.

PREACHER: O heavens! This is ridiculous!

A card is carried from right to left on and off stage, reading:

"O HEAVENS, THIS IS RIDICULOUS!" *says the preacher.*

Mavis scurries into the carriage and seizes up the reins with one hand and holds her umbrella with the other. She motions to TerryBill to join her on the seat nearest the audience, but he hesitates.

Father shouts and points TerryBill to the carriage then points to the sky.

FATHER: Get going. It's raining. *(gesticulating wildly)*

TerryBill shakes his head, seizes the reins with his right hand (of the off-stage unseen horses) from Mavis, gives the reins a flick.

TERRYBILL: *(to the horses)* Gee up there.

The carriage begins to roll as Mavis looks mystified. TerryBill holds onto the carriage with his right hand, moves to the rear of the carriage and begins to run behind the carriage as it rolls slowly off stage.

The wedding party wave goodbye to the couple. TerryBill waves goodbye to both wedding party and to the audience as he and Mavis leave the stage with the carriage.

A card is carried on stage from left, as the storm continues.

The preacher continues to defy the heavens and shakes his fist at the storm. The witnesses begin to witness with vigor. The band strikes up in defiance of the weather. Father sighs and heads for the farmhouse, beckoning the others to follow him. The lights blink and come on again and again as thunder rumbles around.

The card reads:

"AND SO THE STORY OF A TRUE STAND-UP COMEDIAN, RAINS AND THUNDERS TO A SORE BUT HAPPY END."

The card is carried off right as.

Curtain

END OF PLAYSCRIPT

HOPE AND GO SEEK

A Short Story and a
One-Act Playscript

The Story

Once upon a time there were three young prospectors, Hardwork Harry, Hopeful Hal and Honest Hank. They wore broad-brimmed hats and old clothes as they toiled away, searching for gold year after year, in the bitter backwoods of the remotest mountains.

Said Hopeful dreamily, "These mountains lie somewhere in the great outback far along the lonesome and little known trails of the mind."

Hardwork added, "These trails lead to certain success or total failure. Here there can be no in-between, half-way home, no safe retreat."

Honest sighed, "Here, there is only gold and bold riches or useless toil, foul soil and the coil of the snake."

"Yes," said Hopeful, "This is a place to which any man's dreams might one day drive him, a fortress for only the brave, a graveyard of virtually certain dry bones and death at the end of the trail."

"Why would any man come there?" added Hardwork Harry.

"Only because job slavery and sycophancy and seeking after security are even worse," answered Honest Hank. "Yes, the bad choices in this life are there, like rotten fruit for the easy plucking but seems like the good choices - the good fruit - lie high up in an exotic orchard, out of reach, beyond the grasp of any ordinary guy."

The three good, young fellows thought about this for a while.

"Well," said Honest Hank, "after just a few years of this, I'm beginning to see that we're running out of food and drink and house and energy and medicine and money."

"True, indeed," agreed Hopeful Hal, "we have gone to the end of the trail and followed single-minded honesty and hope and hard work. We've gone as far as creative ideas can lead us and we've found nothing . . . At least so far . . ." he added wistfully.

And all three of the young prospectors became sad and philosophical as they peered into the darkness beyond their campfire and saw the shadows of wasted years thinly shimmering beyond the fire's fainting illusions of soon success.

Honest said sadly, "See there in the campfire's flames, the faces of old friends are frowning and the faces of former foes are filled with a loathsome joy."

Each of the young prospectors had come out to the hills by his own unique path and so each one saw something different in the shadows and in the light.

Of the three, by far the greatest believer in honest toil was Hardwork Harry. The one who was most surprised at their failure was the idealist - Hopeful Hal. The most confused and least able to explain their dead-end was Honest Hank who had always believed that honesty was the best policy.

So, on that evening, the three goldbugs sat around their campfire drinking stream water and eating beans and stewed rabbit out of aluminum dishes.

Feeling that they were all in a mood to reminisce and philosophize, Hardwork Harry remarked thoughtfully. "I wonder where did we go wrong in this life? We've all worked hard and yet we've found nothing but work rock. My dad always said, 'Work hard and you will surely succeed.' Perhaps dads don't have all the wisdom. My dad worked hard and yet he never got on well in the world."

Hopeful Hal shook his head, "My old uncle used to say, 'Think Big – that's the key to success.' So I thought big and here I am a real big fat, flat failure."

Honest Hank agreed, "You know, the advice that they throw at you, in school graduation, is very strange really. Our good old wise teachers always advised us that honesty is the best policy. Well we've done honest work - what could be more honest than shoveling and pick-axing for gold - with our own hands - all by the sweat of our brow? And where are we? All the rogues I know are flourishing like wild and wily weeds. Well, I mean, what about all the oldest advice you get, be dedicated, devoted, believe in true love, use your brains and study hard? We've all tried to tread these stony roads. So, if you do these things, how can you end up broke? Or is there a missing link? Something people can't or won't or don't tell you - a secret that they keep for themselves."

"Like what?" asked Hal, scratching his beard furiously. "Genius? Or maybe a great education?"

"What about just plain old patience?" asked Harry.

"No, no, no, I say no to all that be-a-good-boy-and-you'll-do-well nonsense," said Honest Hank, "I insist on being a bad boy - it's my only hope for success.

"I'm thinking of something entirely different from goodboyism - a force we can't even control, that is completely outside of ourselves - fate, fortune, destiny, luck. That's the thing. That's what we need - luck."

"Well, where do we find it? How do we get it?" asked Hardwork Harry.

"The only way I know," said Hopeful Hal, "is to pray for it, work for it, hope for it but however or wherever you find it or don't find it now or never find it that's what we need - the only true secret of success - LUCK."

"Listen," answered Harry, "we've been looking for gold all these years - that's a kind of hard, glinting, shining LUCK. If we can't find gold, how can we find luck?"

"Furthermore," agreed Hal, wagging a finger at Harry, "If we were lucky people we'd have found gold long ago. There's no point in looking for Luck. Luck would find us just as we are sitting here - if we were lucky people."

"Luck, luck, come and find us. We're here," cried Harry, loudly into the hilly forest. His voice echoed.

"LUCK, LUCK, LUCK," cried the spirit of the hills and fainter . . .

"Luck, Luck, Luck."

"Here's someone coming," said Honest.

"Maybe it's luck," cried Hopeful.

"Maybe it's a bandit, let's stand aside and ambush him," Hardwork rallied.

As the three young prospectors slid silently into the shadows, a tall, slim, bearded backpacker leaning on a stout staff, entered the clearing and began poking around with his stick.

"Whatderee poking and sniffing around here for," asked Hank suspiciously as the three young goldbugs sidled carefully out of the shadows.

"Ah, my good friends, nice to meet you. I'm Professor Stargazer. I'm here to observe the heavens from this wonderful vantage point, this panoramic pinnacle of astronomical advantage . . ."

"Very pretty speech," growled Hal, "but why not go to look at the stars somewhere down there? Why up here, in our little lonely spot?"

"As I said - up here for a better view," said the professor.

"Oh, so that was what you meant to say," muttered Honest Hank, "why couldn't you just say so in plain lingo?"

"What - speaking plainly - and lose my lucrative professorship with all its bank balancing bonus and pecuniary perquisites. Ha, ha, plain lingo, indeed. Not a chance," declared the professor. "That would never get a fellah tenure."

"Well, why don't you just go up, up thatta there mountain?" said Hal, "You can see for a million miles from the top of the hill."

"Sir, I am a man of more than threescore years and ten. I need rest. Am I not welcome here? Have you found gold and do not wish me to know?" asked the professor. "I assure you I am silence and secrecy personified. No amount of torture or tribulation or titillation would ever induce me to reveal your secret. They could put me on the rack itself and turn it so mercilessly that . . ."

"O save yourself all the pains and aches, professor. There's nothing to reveal. We're broke . . ." muttered Hank, despondently.

"You might as well sit down and drink some spring water. Here, have a few beans, too, stranger - it's almost about all that's left," invited Hardwork Harry.

"If there's beans going, can I have a share?" asked another voice, as a short, broad man stepped out of the shadows.

"I'm Georgie S. Grubbingrabber," said the second stranger in a friendly way, shaking hands all around. "Trust me, you guys, for a square deal. That's what most folks call me Squaredeal - that's my middle name."

The three goldbugs looked at each other, shrugged, puzzled.

Honest Hank was mystified "A square deal on what? We've nothing to sell."

"Of course you have, my dear young fellahs. That's where you're wrong. You could get a pretty penny for this quaint old mine, you know. A place like this could be rented out to holidaymakers. Why, I could show the suckers, I mean tourists, around here for heap plenty good baubles. Of course, I know there's no gold here - nobody ever finds gold nowadays but I could sure pack in the gawkers and gapers. You see I sell dreams - dreams are worth good money."

"Well, this place ain't for sale, so forget it," said Harry.

"And we don't need no tourists neither stepping nor stomping around here," said Hal.

"They would interfere with the gold digging, not to mention their spying and reporting," added Hank.

"No, no, of course not, visitors would be a menace to you all," agreed Squaredeal. "I meant to buy you boys out so that you could try something else - like an honest trade for instance. Ha. Ha. How's that?"

"You want us to go panhandling, scrounging, begging, thieving? It doesn't sound like a square deal to me," said Hopeful.

Squaredeal sat down with a small plate of beans and began to eat ravenously. "Think about it, boys. There's no hurry for a quick decision. How about a lump sum and a good job working for a mining company? I could get that for you. No problem. A paycheck every month. Gee, what about earning enough to buy a small house in a mere 50 years run or a nice little car to help you go buy the groceries."

"Here, just a minute, Squaredeal, are you trying to buy us out with good jobs? We don't want jobs. We came out here because we all believed that truly there is no such thing as a good job," said Hank.

"A regular paycheck puts you in the way of meeting some real good people," Georgie assured them.

"You've got to be kidding," said Honest.

"That's all I need," cried Hardwork cynically.

"I have met all the people I ever want to meet, in this life," cried Hopeful. "And good riddance to them all."

"I say, a shotgun is the best neighbor," added Hopeful.

"You need money," insisted Grubbingrabber. "You've got to eat."

Georgie was wide-eyed with unbelief.

"Food? We don't need to buy food," said Harry. "It's all here for free - snakes, rabbits, berries, raw beans, wild birds, cacti - not a great variety but all good food."

"Yes, but think about it," said Georgie, "- a TV in your living room! Here, you don't even have a living room never mind a TV in it."

"Just a TV in the living room?" asked Hardwork.

"No, no, no, of course not - chairs and all," said Squaredeal. "You'd have all conceivable helps and gadgets. Piped water, electric lights, windows to see through . . ."

"Yes," said Hank, "windows to see who's coming."

"To arrest us, rob us, murder us or bore us to death . . Yes I see," said Harry.

Hal laughed, "Oh yes, windows."

But Squaredeal assured them keenly, "It's great to have all your comforts. It's a hard life here."

"Here we have all the running water, all the starlight, all the views free. Lookee see here, stranger, Mr. Squaredeal, what you are talking about is just what we all ran away from - safety, security, jobs, slavery, fear of losing the paycheck, being terrorized by the boss crawling and cringing. Yessir, nosir, three bags full sir. That's not a life - that's a sentence to fear for life," cried Hopeful.

"Yessir to you Hopeful and Nosir to you Mr. Squaredeal," agreed Hardwork.

Hank addressed the thin stranger who had been listening without comment, "What do you think, professor? Should we bail out or hang around here some more?"

The slim long-legged professor poked around in the dirt, as he considered the question. "Let's think," he said. So they all sat around the fire.

They looked into the flames and old memories and hopes arose out of the flames.

Still looking far into the distance, the professor spoke, "As a teacher I always advise my students to persevere. It's one of the standard icons of pedagogy. So, stick it out, hang in there and . . er . . so on."

Squaredeal looked confused, thought about it, then muttered, "O yes. I see what you're saying."

"You can't see what he says. You mean you can hear what he says," pointed out Honest Hank.

"Well, whatever, anyway. My advice to you all goldbugs is to sell out and become predictable professionals like the rest of us," said Squaredeal. "Enjoy the good things of life, like music, plays, stories."

Hopeful was astonished and jumped up and stomped his feet. "But why do those things have to be laid out on a plate and paid for so dearly in your silly world here. We sing to ourselves, we tell stories to each other and we dream up plays about what we would do if . . ."

"Let us practice those perambulations sometime soon," yawned the professor. "Meanwhile, I'm going to secure some somnolence."

"He means snatch some sleep," said Honest.

"Oh, no, anything but that," cried Georgie.

"Why, no?" asked Hopeful.

"No one should ever sleep," said Squaredeal, "unless he is prepared to die. See, no one can ever be sure if he will waken up."

However, they all ignored Georgie S. Grubbingrabber and one by one they all fell asleep.

As the others slept, Squaredeal opened up first one eye and then another, rose and began to mutter and search and surreptitiously rummage around. First, he found a few trinkets and stuck a few tools and utensils in his backpack. Soon he found their watches and clocks, held them up in the air, sniggering, rubbing his hands and jumping for joy.

"Ah, ha, this is what I really want - their timepieces - their time," he chortled and giggled as he sneaked off into the shadows.

The others continued to sleep for a while, until a faint light crept up above the western hills and revealed a still shadowy and bleak old mine. A mine that had strangely become dusty and rusty and creaky and leaky - the fire, long since gone out and grown over. Only the crude brick fireplace remained and even it had become grown over with moss and grass.

Hal was the first to waken up. He looked around in fear and confusion. He stretched his limbs. They ached and pained as he moved around. He felt his neck. His hair and beard were bushy and thick and gray. He looked at the back of his hands.

"What's happening?" cried Hal.

Slowly and stiffly the others got up and creaked and moaned and groaned.

"What's going on?" they asked each other - dreading the answer, as they rekindled the fire and shivered in the dark cold and thin dawn.

"You look so old."

"It's only the faint dawn light."

"No, you're 40 or 50 years older."

"Last night I felt like 23 and now I feel like 60 or 73."

The slim professor had by now wakened up and was stretching his limbs. He didn't look any older than the night before but then tall, thin people usually age better than the short and stocky.

"What's happened to us, professor?" asked Hardwork. "How long have we been sleeping? It feels like decades."

The professor looked at his watch, "Decades? Rubbish! We've all been asleep about eight hours, indeed seven hours and forty six minutes precisely."

"Then why do we feel more like 70?" asked Harry.

"Why is our mine mossed over?" asked Hank.

"Why has our hair turned gray even on our hands?" asked Hal.

"Don't you see it. Don't you see why?" cried the thin man. "It's your own fault. You entertained a liar - George S. Grubbingrabber - who has stolen everything he could lay his thieving hands on - including your time. He's off with - judging by your appearances - about 40 years of your lives. I could work out the exact amount mentally if you give me a moment. Let me see, now - yes exactly 48 years, six months, five days, three hours and 32 seconds. That's precisely what he stole of your lives."

"Just a minute now, professor. How do you know that, that exact amount? Just who are you?"

asked Hank, "Is this a joke? What are you? Is this a dream? What's your name?"

"O yes, I told you my profession. I forgot to mention my full name. Professor Stargazer N. Luck. N for numbers. I'm the one you summoned from the echo and the echo called me. Remember?"

"No. I don't believe it," said Hardwork Harry.

"You're him, for real?" asked Hopeful Hal.

Honest Hank sighed, "Well here we are, getting old and getting nowhere . . ."

The professor replied, "No one is going nowhere in *my* presence."

"Then perhaps meeting you now has been worth the wait?" said Honest.

"Yes, I'm Professor Luck - the man with all the destiny numbers and the magic pointer."

"But you'll help us?" asked Hopeful.

"Yes, of course," replied the professor. "I'm always willing to give *at least a little* help to the hardworking, the honest, the hopeful. You should have sent for me sooner."

The professor poked his lightie-up stick at the three old goldbugs. "I can't bring back your stolen time but I can give you the luck of healthy and vigorous old bones."

The stick glowed like a star and the three goldbugs began to dance around like three year-olds, crying, "Luck. Luck. Professor Luck has come at last."

And then the three goldbugs spoke more slowly and soberly. . . "Alas, alas, the torments and tortures of youth are all gone away."

The professor pointed his stick at some of the high rocks nearby and jumped around and danced and cried, "There's gold. See gold - more gold - all you need to do is break it up, sluice it and drink it. There's millions in gold around you."

"Drink it, professor? Don't you mean sell it?" asked Hal.

"Not that kind of gold, my three good friends," replied the professor. "In that rock there is now liquid gold - the elixir of wisdom. That will help you to be wise and understand life and death and those things in between and friend and foe - who is true and who is mere deceiver. Never again will you trust a Squaredeal."

The three goldbugs danced around Professor Luck in joy and song.

Then the professor cried, "Only discernment and wisdom and straight thinking stands between you and a life of clear outsight and inmost understanding."

Hardwork Hal beamed, "Any kind of gold is success and will certainly do me."

Honest cried, "That magic gold juice of wisdom and luck is a winning combination and bound to throw up a few dollars now and again."

Then they all danced around the fire and Hopeful pointed to the fire and said, "See in the flames the faces of old friends filled with love and laughing and the faces of former foes frowning and cast down with disappointment."

Hardwork cried, "See up there, the sun struggles free from his nightchains and drags his face up out of the far hills."

Then Hopeful cried, "And hear the high blue dawnbird beginning to sing a new song that no one has ever heard before."

Then the tall man slowly slipped into the trees, waving his magic stick to the goldbugs and calling out, "I must travel on. I hear someone else trying and crying for me out there."

Professor Luck disappeared into the shortening shadows of the daybreak that crept slowly up upon the old camp and mine.

Honest asked, "Where has Professor Luck gone?"

And Hopeful answered him, "Out there into the great winds and forests and rivers and seas."

Hardwork looked far into the distance, "Yes, and there he is still - wandering at his will with his magic stick and destiny numbers, alive and willing to help those who have courage and goodness and faith, somewhere out there far along the little known and lonesome trails of the mind."

END OF STORY

The Playscript
A Slapstick Comedy In One Act

Hardwork Harry)
Hopeful Hal) Gold prospectors
Honest Hank)
Professor Stargazer N. Luck – A man of magic and a foreteller of fortunes
Georgie S. Grubbingrabber – A city slicker and businessman
Three Simple Songs: *Gold Bugs; the Squirrel Song; What a Good Dog I Will Be*
Scene – Out in them thar hills

****

SCENE ONE

Outside an old mine, set in the wooded hills, is a clearing with a creek flowing through it and an old stone fireplace in the center, around which there are scattered logs to serve as seats. A few tools and utensils are lying around here and there.

Sitting there are three young prospectors, Hardwork Harry, Hopeful Hal, Honest Hank, all dressed in broad-brimmed hats and old clothes. For the past few years they have been toiling away, searching for gold, in the backwoods of the remotest mountains. Now they are reminiscing. They all march around the stage, singing

GOLD BUGS

Sung: Jerkily and Cheerfully

VERSE 1:
d f l f d f l f
We shovel and slave, we rant and rave
d - d f f f m r m f s
As we scratch each patch for the wealth we crave
d f l f d f l f
Ho, ho, hee, hee, ho, ho, hee, hee
l d^1 l s s f
We'll bug all day for gold
d f l - l f d f l f
It's more than a joke, we've all gone broke
d f f - f - f m - r m - f s
It's not just a fad, we're raving mad
d f l f d f l f
Ho, ho, hee, hee, ho, ho, hee, hee
l d^1 l s s f
We'll bug all day for gold

Verse 1:
We shovel and slave, we rant and rave
As we scratch each patch for the wealth we crave
Ho, ho, hee, hee, ho, ho, hee, hee
We'll dig all day for gold
It's more than a joke, we've all gone broke
It's not just a fad, we're raving mad
Ho, ho, hee, hee, ho, ho, hee, hee
We'll dig all day for gold.

Refrain:
Some little bugs come, some big bugs go
That's just the way of the world you know
But the only bugs who never grow old
Are the bugs who burrow for gold
Smash up the stones, give them a kick
One more shovel load might do the trick
Ho, ho, hee, hee, ho, ho, hee, hee
We dig and burrow for gold.

Verse 2:
And when we've found the gold we love
We'll dig some more for treasure trove
Ho, ho, hee, hee, ho, ho, hee, hee
We'll dig for treasure trove
The search for treasure never ends
We may strut all around and impress our friends
Ho, ho, hee, hee, ho, ho, hee, hee
Then we'll dig for treasure trove.

Verse 3:
If you live in hope you'll never grow old
It'll keep you alive just a digging for gold
Ho, ho, hee, hee, ho, ho, hee, hee
We'll dig for silver and gold
But when we've made our very last "try"
We'll dig some more in the sweet bye and bye
Ho, ho, hee, hee, ho, ho, hee, hee
We're bugs for treasure trove.

HAL: *(dreamily)* Sometimes I wonder if these mountains are real. It's like they lie somewhere in the great outback far along the lonesome and little known trails of the mind. What an otherworldly place!

HARRY: Yes, these are trails that lead to certain success or total failure. Here there can be no in-between, half-way home, no safe retreat.

HANK: *(sighing)* Yip, there is only gold or silver or treasure trove or useless toil, foul soil and the coil of the snake.

HARRY: Yet this is a landscape where any traveling man's dreams might one day drive him, a fortress for only the brave, a graveyard of virtually certain dry bones and death at the end of the trail. I've often wondered, why would any man come there?

HANK: Well, job slaves are spit licking and crawling after the boss-man. Grubbing and grabbing after paychecks is like chasing a ghost, a phantom, smoke and mirrors. Now you see it - then it's gone. All the bad choices in this life are there, like rotten fruit for easy plucking but it seems like the good choices - the good fruit, lies high up in a rare orchard, out of reach, far beyond the grasp of you or me.

HAL: We've gone as far as our hard work can take us and we've found nothing . . at least so far . . .

All three of the young prospectors become sad and philosophical as they see the darkness out there beyond their campfire.

HANK: *(sadly)* I see the shadows of wasted years thinly shimmering beyond the fire's fainting illusions of soon success. See there in the campfire's flames, the faces of old friends are frowning and the faces of former foes are filled with a loathsome joy.

HAL: Each of us has come out here along his own path, so each of us is bound to see something different in the shadows and in the light. You are the one who trusted honest toil - Hardwork Harry.

I am the one who is most surprised at our failure. That's why you call me - Hopeful Hal. *(he smiles)* And you, Honest Hank, you have always believed that honesty is the best policy.

HARRY: So, maybe this evening, we should all just sit around the campfire. We'll drink good old creek water and eat beans and stewed rabbit. *(he sets aside some aluminum dishes)* Not a high class meal - I'm afraid.

HAL: *(thoughtfully)* Indeed, the very idea makes me wonder where did we go wrong in this life? We've all worked hard and yet we've found nothing but work rock. My dad always said, 'Work hard and you will surely succeed.' Perhaps dads don't have all the wisdom. My dad worked hard and yet he never got on well in the world.

HANK: *(shaking his head)* My old uncle used to say, 'Think Big' – that's the key to success. So I thought big and here I am a real big fat, flat failure.

You know, the advice that they throw at you, in school graduation, is very strange really. Our good old wise teachers always advised us that honesty is the best policy. Well, we've done honest work. What could be more honest than shoveling and pick-axing for treasure - with our own hands - all by the sweat of our brow? And where are we? All the rogues I know are flourishing like wild weeds. *(ironically)* Be dedicated, devoted, use your brains and study hard? We've all tried to tread those stony roads. So, if you do these things, how can you end up broke? Or is there a missing link? I just wonder if there is something people can't or won't or don't tell you - a secret that they keep for themselves.

HARRY: Like what? *(scratching his beard furiously)* Genius? Or maybe a great education?

HAL: *(excitedly)* What about just plain old patience?

HANK: No, no, no, I say no to all that be-a-good-boy-and-you'll-do-well nonsense. I insist on being a bad boy - it's my only hope for success.

I'm thinking of something entirely different from goodboyism - perhaps a force we can't even control, that is completely outside of ourselves - other people, the world, fate, fortune, destiny, luck. That's what we need - luck.

HAL: *(walking up and down agitatedly)* Well, where do we find it?

HARRY: That I do not know but whether you find it or don't find it - now or never – that's what you need - the one and only true secret of success - LUCK.

HANK: Listen, we've been looking for gold or silver or jewels all these years - that's a kind of hard, glinting, shining LUCK. If we can't find treasure trove, how can we find luck?

HAL: Furthermore, *(wagging a finger at Hank)* if we were lucky people we'd have found treasure long ago. There's no point in looking for Luck. Luck would find us just as we are - sitting here - if we were lucky people.

HARRY: *(loudly into the hilly forest, his voice echoing)* Luck, luck, come and find us. We're here.

ECHO: *(the spirit of the hills)* LUCK, LUCK.

LUCK: *(growing fainter)* Luck, Luck, Luck.

HANK: Here's someone coming.

HAL: Maybe it's luck.

HARRY: Maybe it's a bandit, let's stand aside and ambush him.

As the three young prospectors slide silently into the shadows, a tall, slim, bearded older gentleman in white shirt and black coat with tails, enters the clearing and begins poking around with his stick.

HANK: *(suspiciously)* Whatderee poking and sniffing around here for?

The three prospectors sidle carefully out of the shadows.

PROFESSOR STARGAZER: Ah, my good friends - nice to meet you. I'm Professor Stargazer. I'm here to observe the heavens from this wonderful vantage point. This panoramic pinnacle of astronomical advantage.

HAL: *(growling)* Very pretty speech. But why not go to look at the stars somewhere down there? Why up here, in our little lonely spot?

PROFESSOR: As I said - up here for a better view.

HANK: *(muttering)* Oh, so that was what you meant to say. Why couldn't you just say so in plain lingo?

PROFESSOR: What - speak plainly - and lose my lucrative professorship with all its bank balancing bonus and pecuniary perquisites? Ha, ha, plain lingo, indeed. Not a chance. That would never get a fellow tenure.

HARRY: Well, why don't you just go up, up thatta there mountain? You can see for a million miles from the top of the hill.

PROFESSOR: Sir, I am a man of more than threescore years and ten. I need rest. Am I not welcome here? Have you struck gold or silver or other treasure and do not wish me to know? I assure you that I am silence and secrecy personified. No amount of torture or tribulation or titillation would ever induce me to reveal your secret. *(his eyes narrow as he grows intense)* They could put me on the rack itself and turn it so mercilessly that . . .

HANK: *(shaking his head despondently)* O save yourself all the pains and aches, Professor. There's nothing to reveal. We're broke . . .

HARRY: You might as well sit down and drink some creek water. Here, have a few beans, too, stranger - it's about all that's left.

> ***Enter Georgie S. Grubbingrabber**, a short, broad-shouldered man who steps out of the shadows. He is dressed as a dude cowboy in fine western gear.*

GRUBBINGRABBER: If there's beans going, can I have a share? I'm Georgie Grubbingrabber. *(in a friendly way, shaking hands all around)* Trust me, you guys, for a square deal. That's what most folks call me - Squaredeal - that's my middle name.

> *The three goldbugs look at each other and shrug in puzzlement.*

HANK: *(mystified)* A square deal on what? We've nothing to sell - no money to buy.

GRUBBINGRABBER: Of course you have, my dear young fellahs. That's where you're wrong. You could get a pretty penny for this quaint old mine, you know. A place like this could be rented out to holidaymakers. Of course, I know there's no gold here - nobody ever finds gold nowadays but I could sure pack in the gawkers and gapers. You see I sell dreams - dreams are worth good money. And I'm the original cowboy wheelerdealer.

HARRY: *(morosely)* Well, this place ain't for sale, so forget it.

HAL: And we don't need no tourists, neither, stepping nor stomping around here.

HANK: Tourists would interfere with the gold digging, not to mention their spying and reporting.

GRUBBINGRABBER: *(pacifyingly)* No, no, of course not, visitors would be a menace to you all. I mean to buy you boys out completely so that you can try something else - like an honest trade for instance. Ha. Ha. How's that? How's about a steady job?

HAL: A job? You mean you want us to go panhandling, scrounging, begging, thieving? It doesn't sound like a square deal, to me. There's no such thing as a good job. There's no such thing as a good boss. The only good boss is yourself.

Squaredeal sits down with a small plate of beans and begins to eat ravenously.

GRUBBINGRABBER: Think about it, boys. There's no hurry for a quick decision. How about a lump sum up front and a good job working for a chemical company? No problem. A paycheck every month. Gee, what about earning enough to buy a small house in a mere 50 year's time or a nice little car to help you go buy the groceries.

HANK: Here, just a minute, Squaredeal, are you trying to buy us out with regular jobs? We don't want a wage-earning career. We came out here because we all believed that truly there is no such thing as a good paycheck - they all cost too much in stress. Working for a big firm is like buying a lottery ticket. Yes. A few - one or two - a few hit it big - make real money. But the thousands and millions lose their lot - that's what a lottery is - big biz in a swiz with some fun ideas to trick you.

GRUBBINGRABBER: *(reassuringly)* You don't mean to say that you want to BE YOUR OWN BOSS? *(the three goldbugs nod keenly)* Bah! You'll likely starve. And a regular paycheck puts you in the way of meeting some real nice people - you become socially acceptable, see?

HANK: You've got to be kidding.

HARRY: *(cynically)* That's all I need.

HAL: I have met all the people I ever want to meet in this life. And good riddance to them all.

HANK: I have always said that a shotgun is the best neighbor you'll ever have.

GRUBBINGRABBER: *(insisting)* You need money. *(wide-eyed with disbelief)* You've got to eat.

HAL: Food? We don't need to buy food. It's all here for free - snakes, rabbits, berries, raw beans, wild birds, cacti - not a great variety but it's all good food.

GRUBBINGRABBER: Yes, but think about it - a TV in your living room! Here, you don't even have a living room never mind a TV in it. And that's not all. No, no, no, of course not - chairs and all. All conceivable helps and gadgets. Piped water, electric lights, windows to see through . . .

HANK: *(scanning the horizon with hands shading his eyes)* Yes, windows to see who's coming.

HAL: *(laughing)* Yes I see. To arrest us, rob us, murder us or bore us to death . . . Yes I see. Oh yes, windows to let the burglars see in advance what they're getting.

GRUBBINGRABBER: *(assuring them keenly)* Lookee see, fellahs. It's great to have all your comforts. It's a hard life here.

HANK: Here we have all the running water, all the starlight, all the views free. Listen here, stranger, Mr. Squaredeal, what you are talking about is just what we all ran away from - safety, security, jobs, slavery, fear of losing the paycheck, crawling and cringing, being terrorized by the boss. Yessir, nosir, three bags full sir. That's not a life - that's a sentence to fear for life.

HARRY: Yessir to you Hopeful and Nosir to you Mr. Squaredeal. O what good dogs we would have to be to earn our scraps. We'd have to sit up and beg. *(Harry begs like a dog as Hank tumbles and Hal jumps up and down).*

HANK: *(addressing Professor Stargazer who has been listening without comment)* What do you think, Professor? Should we bail out or hang around here some more?

The professor pokes around in the dirt, as he considers the question.

PROFESSOR: Let's think.

They all sit around the fire, looking into the flames.

HAL: I seem to see old memories and hopes rising out of these flames.

PROFESSOR: *(still looking far into the distance)* As a teacher I always advise my students to persevere. It's one of the standard icons of pedagogy. So, stick it out, hang in there and . . er . . so on.

GRUBBINGRABBER: *(looking confused and thoughtful, then muttering)* Well yes. I see what you're saying – but . . .

HANK: You can't see what he says. You mean you can hear what he says.

GRUBBINGRABBER: Well, whatever, anyway. My advice to you all goldbugs is to sell out and become predictable professionals like the rest of us - enjoy the good things of life, like music, plays, stories.

HAL: *(astonished, jumping up and stomping his feet)* But why do those things have to be laid out on a plate and paid for so dearly in your silly world down here? We sing to ourselves, we tell stories to each other and we dream up plays about what we would do if . . .

PROFESSOR: *(yawning)* Let us practice those perambulations sometime soon, meanwhile I'm going to secure some somnolence.

HANK: He means snatch some sleep.

GRUBBINGRABBER: Oh, no, anything but that.

HAL: Why, no?

GRUBBINGRABBER: No one should ever sleep, unless he wants to drop dead. See, no one can ever be sure of wakening up. Besides, that's when the bandits catch you unawares. *(he draws his hand sharply across his throat)* When you sleep, they creep.

They all ignore Georgie S. Grubbingrabber and one by one they all fall asleep. As the others sleep, Squaredeal opens up first one eye and then another, rises and begins to mutter and search and surreptitiously rummage around. First, he finds a few trinkets and sticks a few tools and utensils in his backpack. Soon he finds their small change, watches and clocks, holds them up in the air, sniggering, rubbing his hands and jumping for joy.

GRUBBINGRABBER: Ah, ha, this is what I want most - their timepieces - their time-schemes. *Grubbingrabber chortles and giggles as he sneaks off into the shadows.*
(to audience) I'm not really stealing - only borrowing, yes?

AUDIENCE: *(led by conductor using hand-signs)* No!

GRUBBINGRABBER: *(outraged, to audience)* I'm not a thief, am I?

AUDIENCE: Oh, yes you are.

GRUBBINGRABBER: *(to audience)* Oh no I'm not a thief, not that. I'm just a borrower, right?

AUDIENCE: Oh, no you're not.

GRUBBINGRABBER: Oh, no, no. I am not a rogue, a liar, a thief, am I?

AUDIENCE: Oh, yes you are.

GRUBBINGRABBER: No, no, no.

AUDIENCE: Yes, yes, yes.

GRUBBINGRABBER: *(to audience)* Now, be fair, be honest, tell the truth - what do you really think of me?

AUDIENCE: Boo, boo, boo.

Grubbingrabber panics, falls into the dying embers of the fire then, sparks flying from his clothes, runs off stage left.

The others sigh and moan and toss in their troubled dreams but fitfully continue to sleep for a while. All the lights on stage go out and there is a pause.

Curtain

SCENE TWO

The same scene as before but later in the night. All continue to sleep. Slowly a faint light creeps up above the western hills and reveals a still shadowy and bleak old mine site.

This mine has strangely become dusty and rusty and creaky and leaky - the fire, long since gone out and grown over. Only the crude brick fireplace remains and even it has become grown over with moss and grass.

Hal is the first to waken up. He looks around in fear and confusion. He stretches his limbs. He appears full of aches and pains as he moves around. He touches his neck tenderly. His hair and beard are now bushy and thick and gray. He looks at the back of his hands.

HAL: What's happening?

Slowly and stiffly the others get up, limbs creaking, moaning and groaning.

HARRY: *(nervously)* What's going on?

The others rekindle the fire and shiver in the dark cold and thin dawn. They look each other up and down.

HAL: You look so old.

HARRY: It's only the faint dawn light.

HANK: No, you're 40 or 50 years older.

HAL: Last night I felt like 23 and now I feel like 60 or 73.

The professor has by now wakened up and is stretching his limbs.

HANK: Professor, you don't look any older than the night before.

PROFESSOR: Well, we tall, thin people usually age better than the short and stocky.

HARRY: What is happening, Professor? How long have we been sleeping? It feels like decades.

PROFESSOR: *(looking at his watch)* Decades? Rubbish! We've all been asleep about eight hours, indeed seven hours and forty six minutes precisely.

HARRY: Then why do we feel so old and achy?

HAL: Why is the old mine mossed over?

HANK: Why has our hair turned gray even on our hands?

PROFESSOR: Don't you see it? Don't you see why? It's your own fault. You made friends with a liar - George S. Grubbingrabber. He has stolen everything he could lay his thieving hands on - including your time. He's off with - judging by your appearances - about 40 years of your lives. I could work out the exact amount mentally if you give me a moment. Let me see, now – yes, exactly 38 years, six months, five days, three hours and 32 seconds. That's precisely what he has stolen of your lives.

HARRY: I would never have believed it possible *(exercising his arms and shoulders)* except that I feel so old.

HAL: Me too. And I can see you look the way I feel. It must be true as the professor says. We've grown old.

PROFESSOR: This is a horrible place. I'm taking a walk. Cherrio, chaps.

HAL, HARRY AND HANK: Oh, ta, ta, old boy.

Exit the Professor.

The three bugs shake their heads and shrug.

HANK: It's all so insane. I don't believe it. Heck. I wish I'd never come here. I well remember the day I graduated from college. The speaker was a distinguished educator *(imitating the speaker with a supercilious and patronizing air)* "and finally as you leave this our beautiful graduation ceremony and go to take your places out in the real world, I would finally enjoin you . . what you become is entirely in your own hands.

"The world is there for your taking. Of course, this will require honest toil on your part but armed with the bright torch of knowledge and innovation, sustained by self faith in your ability, supported by the true love of your devoted friends and family - you can do it.

"Always remember to say to yourself over and over again - I can do it, I will do it, yes I will truly succeed. Life is a garden. I will pluck the flowers. Yes, dear graduates - it all depends on you."

(bitterly) What a garbage heap of lies from first to last - the truth is the exact opposite - it all depends on other people - like Georgie S. Grubbingrabber, for instance and dozens and thousands and millions of others.

Hank bows sarcastically.

HAL: *(glumly)* Yes, I had the same experience. My teachers always said *(in a squeaky supercilious voice)* "Have high hopes and you'll get ahead." So I set my sights high and here I am - a bum.

HANK: My poor old mother was a great believer in truth. *(affecting a maternal posture and wagging his fingers)* She said, "Always tell the truth." So - here I am still truthtelling as I see it . . but nothing happens. *(sighs)* Except that I get robbed by Mr. Squaredeal when I'm asleep!

HAL: Still, he did warn us against it.

HANK: Against what?

HAL: Sleep.

HANK: Oh . . . O yes.

HARRY: You know, fellahs, what we need is luck. I've come to the conclusion that it's not all up to us - the way they tell it at the graduation kick-you-out ceremonies - all that gas is just to put the blame on you instead of on their bad teaching. Mostly it's a matter of luck, people you meet - the world around you.

HANK: *(shaking his head)* If the gold or silver or precious stones aren't here, all the digging in the world won't find any. We need something to bring us luck - a lucky charm for a lucky break.

HARRY: Right you are - some people are born lucky. Not us, after four years grime-grubbing there's still no sign of the glittering gleam.

HAL: And we've had more rabbits paws in the stew here than the rattlesnakes. I don't know of any way to get luck - except maybe to hope for it, but I dunno.

HARRY: Yes, if we had luck we wouldn't need to hoke and poke, we'd just find treasure, just like that. *(snapping his fingers)*

I well remember an old legend in these hills that the King Gold Bug - a kind of lucky spirit of the forests - travels about by night and puts a magic spell on certain rocks and streams - touches them with his golden wand and *(pauses at a loss/shrugs)* and that's where the gold or treasure comes from . . I think . . see, it's all a matter for other people. If the Gold Bug King touches it, it wins - if he doesn't, it doesn't.

HAL: *(shaking his head)* Ah, that's all a fairy tale. Maybe, it's all a matter of faith and positive thoughts after all. As for me, I'll never give up . . there's nothing else to life really than to keep trying.

HARRY: Yes, if we could just keep on working like the squirrels here, we'll hit paydirt sooner or later – that's what I always say. Those little critters sure keep on working all the time . . .

HANK: Cheer up - I say a long chat with the old professor will make us feel better. Seems like he's here to philosophize and figure things out. Why don't we just shoot the breeze with him. And besides, if he's interested in gold - the old professor - would like to invest a few thousand in our diggings and panning here - it would help to keep us going for a couple more years.

HAL: Now you're talking, Hank. I like that idea.

HARRY: *(nodding)* Yea, I couldn't think of a better investment for a traveling man - like the professor.

HAL: *(surprised)* Really? Meaning if he keeps traveling he might forget about the investment, eh? A good investment? Us?

HANK: This old mine is good enough for us and it's good enough for some old city slicker, that's what I say. But you'll need to clean up, Harry, if you want to attract investors.

HAL: Hssh. *(jerks thumb in direction of offstage and then continues eating beans industriously as one unaware of anyone approaching)*

HARRY: *(indignantly)* What do you mean, clean up?

HANK: Why don't you have a bath? A bath, a good wash, see? I can't stand the stink of you anymore!

HARRY: What and risk catching a chill! I'd rather be dirty and have my health.

HANK: We agreed to wash once a week in the interests of friendship, that is so as not to stink and your week is up tonight, O.K.?

HARRY: Well I have to conserve our soap. If I wash tonight I'll clean up only seven day's dirt and filthy sweat, but if I save up another day's dirt I'll get eight days dirt off for the same amount of soap, see? Let's be thrifty. This is a business, all right? Remember? A business deal O.K. See? *(nods significantly)* Save money.

HAL: Oh, all right, you two. Wrap it up.

Enter the Professor *he is still dressed as an old-fashioned city gentleman with a string tie.*

The prospectors stand up and make him welcome - offer beans.

HARRY: Come on in, make yourself at home, have some beans. Did you like the look of these parts? Tell us Professor. You believe we can hit the glittering gleam one day - with your help, of course?

PROFESSOR: *(dreamily)* Ah, yes, the endless search of man for the fountain of eternal . . youth did you say? Oh yes.

HAL: Then done - agreed - for just 10,000; All right, Harry. O.K. Hank? *(slaps his knee in agreement of a deal)*

HARRY AND HANK: Right, it's a bargain.

PROFESSOR: *(at a loss)* What's a bargain?

HANK: We've just made you a 1/4 equal partner for only 10,000. Is it a deal?

PROFESSOR: *(shaking his head and laughing)* Sure thing! I can't think of a better place or a better way to spend my money. Well, yes, I've always liked the idea of being my own boss. *(writes on a piece of paper)* Here's my check. Let's all be goldbugs together.

HARRY: It's heart-breaking to think that somewhere out there in the forest and hills, the King Gold Bug is traveling through and touching the rocks with his magic walking stick - destined to be found by some lucky prospector.

Perhaps a band of his followers - the little forest silver bugs - the elves of the dig - are dancing on a secret mine somewhere out there in the hills and woods just a little ways away - and yet so far - if only we knew where. I can just picture their dancing toes as they jump for joy and dig for gold or silver.

HANK: Oh, that's all a fairy tale, just part of the lore of the old prospector, like the tale of the Lost Dutchman's Mine. There's no such person as the King Gold Bug or his band of elfin gold diggers . . . I'm pretty sure. We just have to keep digging. But it's hard and dirty and mucky work. Smelly work. *(nodding significantly)* Ain't it, Harry?

PROFESSOR: Yes, Harry. Why not wash once in a year or two?

HARRY: Wash? Me wash? What a notion.

PROFESSOR: Oh yes, washing is good, I do believe. Yes, it's a good thing for sure.

HARRY: Now, some folks holds as it's dangerous to your health but no. No way I say. Even if it's a danger to health, I don't mind. All life is a chance. Ain't it? Still, tell me Professor do you believe in thrift?

PROFESSOR: Sure. Thrift is fine.

HARRY: You do? Me too. Put it here. *(puts out his hand and shakes the professor's hand)* See, it's like this . . I'm trying to be thrifty. I'm saving up the dirt on me for another week or two and then washing it all off with just one bar of soap. See that's thriftiness - not dirtyness. See, all those forest animals don't use no soap and they are all clean.

PROFESSOR: *(shaking his head in sympathy)* Yes, I agree. I just wish you all could find what you're looking for as easily as some of these woodland critters all around us. Why it should be as easy for you as it is for a squirrel finding a nut or a bird finding a worm.

HARRY: How come we're smarter than they are but we can't do what they do? Yep - these critters sure could give us a lesson.

HANK: Well, they ain't smart enough to tell us how they do it but we're smart enough to watch'em.

HAL: Yes, if we are going to find or scratch or dig something good out of these here hills, we need to lookee see how those smart little critters do it.

Hal leads as they all sing SQUIRREL and dance around in the firelight.

SQUIRREL

Sung: Rollicking

VERSE 1:
m m m - m m m - m
I'd like to be a squirrel
m r - d d r - d
A-jumping high and low
m s - s l s - s m - m
He always finds a way to get
f s - s f m – r
To where he wants to go
m f s - s l - s - s s – m
Now, if such a skittery critter
m - f s - s m d - r
Can find a way that's new
d - r m - m s_1 - s_1 l_1 d - d
Then we can skip the crumbling dreams
m r d - d d - d
And find our own way through

Verse 1:
I'd like to be a squirrel
A-jumping high and low
He always finds a way to get
To where he wants to go
Now, if such a skittery critter
Can find a way that's new
Then we can skip the crumbling dreams
And find our own way through

REFRAIN:
d r m - m - m m - m - m m - m
O the squirrelly - iddelly-iddel
m - m r - d d d - d
Goes a bouncing with a bump
m s - s l - s - s s - m
Through bushes into the middle
f - f s - s - s f - m - m r
With a jittery, flittery jump
m f s - s - s - l s - s - s - m
He's a trickery-dick and a riddle
m s s m d r
He's there and then he's gone
d r m - m - m m - m - m m - m
For the squirrelly - iddelly-iddel
m m r - d - d d - d - d d
Goes a squirrelly- iddeling on

Refrain:
O the squirrelly-iddelly-iddel
Goes a bouncing with a bump
Through bushes into the middle
With a jittery, flittery jump
He's a trickery-dick and a riddle
He's there and then he's gone
For the squirrelly-iddelly-iddel
Goes a squirrelly-iddeling on.

Verse 2::
Now the squirrel has a passport
That always gets him by
It's a slippery zippery bluster
And it makes his engines fly
Though the woods are slick and thickety
And weeds are worrying high
We'll dig the good things out of the hills
If we give it a squirrelly try.

PROFESSOR: What a great place to look for golden or silver landscapes. There's plenty of them, here.

HARRY: We just need the gold and silver and never mind the landscapes but sure enough, there's a lot of hard work has disappeared into the ground here.

HANK: But nothing comes back out. *(shakes head)* All we do is grub like bugs for buried treasure.

PROFESSOR: Well – that's hard graft and I am glad to hear about all your hard work, my dear chaps. Why, that's one of the great foundations of our civilization. Work hard, tell the truth, be hopeful and positive, use your brains – that's the road to success - right?

The three prospectors fall all over the place and laugh and laugh!

HAL: No, no, Professor. Hope and enthusiasm and hard work and honesty have always been the three surest ways to fail or get fired from any job.

HANK: They're the three worst things you could do - except, perhaps, for having brains. These are the top three reasons for failure in life. So, just say no to more Hardwork, Hope and Honesty and you'll do well in the world.

HANK: Well, Professor. What do you think?

PROFESSOR: Of hopefulness, hard work, honesty? Well, these are things that I used to recommend to my pupils. When I'm asked to give advice, I tell my students - if you want to succeed, follow the open road - be hopeful, optimistic and people will like your hard work and you'll get promotion; be honest and your fellows will respect you, use your brains, be honest and you'll succeed.

But with these hard luck stories you've given me a lot to think about. It's getting late so I'll just go out into the woods and mull it over while I enjoy the night airs.

Exit Professor.

The three treasure bugs bed down and slowly fall into deep snoring sleeps. There are night sounds such as owls, crickets and coyotes.

Enter Georgie S. Grubbingrabber, *now dressed as a lumberjack in checked shirt and jeans with an axe in his hand. Stealthily, he creeps past the bugs and begins to hack with his axe at some of the mine machinery in the shadows. He sniggers and chortles.*

GRUBBINBRABBER: This'll let them know the problems of being self-employed.

Wood cracks and splits and the sound almost awakens the three prospectors. He swings his axe again and again and there is the loud crunch of breaking wood and smashing metal. The three treasure bugs now waken up fully with a start and cry out. They rise up.

HAL: What was that noise?

HARRY: Sounded like a tree falling.

HANK: *(puzzled)* More like metal breaking.

Grubbingrabber steps into the light of the fire.

GRUBBINGRABBER: *(swinging his axe on his shoulder)* I was just breaking up some firewood for you old pals of mine.

HANK: Oh, it's you again. Since when did you want to help anyone, Mr. Bossman?

GRUBBINGRABBER: Oh, come on. Hello fellahs. Let's be pals. *(ingratiatingly)* I'm your old pal Squaredeal, but you can call me Georgie, this time. I was just waiting until that old weirdo went away. I don't trust anyone who says he's a professor. Who does he think he's kidding?

The three treasure bugs are astonished.

HAL: You're a rogue. What are you up to?

HARRY: You scoundrel, you liar.

HANK: The thief of time.

GRUBBINGRABBER: Thief of time? I don't get it. I never stole anything in my life.

HAL: You stole 40 years of our life.

Grubbingrabber laughs and laughs and shakes his head.

HANK: And some of our gear and pots and pans and odds and ends and small change as well.

HAL: Not to mention our goods and chattels.

GRUBBINGRABBER: *(outraged)* How could I do all that, I, a poor, simple cowboy wheeler-dealer and honest tree-chopper? How could I steal 40 years of your lives? Anyone, anyone will tell you that just ain't possible. That's fantasy. And stealing your goods? Who, who, I'd like to know, told you that? Who had the gall, the mendacity, the filth of mind to accuse ME, me an honest, hardworking, decent soul? WHO had the effrontery to accuse me, me, of being the lowest form of scum, the lowest of the low - a petty thief, a small-time crook? Never in my life have I been so humiliated and wronged by being accused of stealing miserable pennies. Why, if I ever wanted to lose my hard-earned reputation for honesty and decency - I would steal a million not your silly old pots and pans and tools and small change. Not that I ever would rob or steal but grant me, credit me, with the common sense at least, to steal something big and worthwhile.

HARRY: Yes . . like the best part of our lives, for instance.

GRUBBINGRABBER: *(laughing again and shaking his head)* One more time - that ain't no go, noways. Only you can spend your lives, nobody else can steal time, the way you say. Who told you that cock and bull story? WHO? I want to know. My good name counts to me. I demand to know . . . Who is my accuser . . eh?

Grubbingrabber clenches his fist and glowers from one to another. The three bugs look sheepishly at each other. Hank digs his foot in the ground and appears to be worried.

HANK: *(to the other two bugs)* I suppose we need to tell him?

Hal and Harry sadly nod their heads.

HANK: Well it was the Prof. Professor Luck.

GRUBBINGRABBER: *(with outrage)* Him, that old fraud. He knows nothing. He's a deceiver, a cheat, a rogue. I wondered what he was up to, poking around here. . . Did he get money from you?

HAL: No, just the opposite. He gave money to US.

GRUBBINGRABBER: He gave you money - I don't believe it. He gave you money with no strings attached . . ?

HANK: *(reluctantly)* Well . . not exactly, we sold him a 25% interest in our mine.

GRUBBINGRABBER: *(mouth open, gaping in disbelief)* For how much?

HANK: 10,000.

GRUBBINGRABBER: 10,000 - you gave away a quarter of this great mine for just 10,000. Mark my words, there'll come a time when this mine will earn as much in a week. *(nodding his head thoughtfully)*

So that's what he was up to - hmm - snooping around and lying about decent old Georgie Squaredeal Grubbingrabber. Ah . . so that's it. He robbed you of a big chunk of your life's work. Why, the squaredeal I offered you would have paid you off with getting you a small down payment admittedly but you would have gotten a big fat paycheck every month for life. Boy, were you boys taken in by that old ripper-offer. *(aggressively)* How could you have believed him against me?

HARRY: *(looking Grubbingrabber up and down suspiciously)* Well, we quite like the old professor and besides we all felt like 40 years older after you left.

HAL: *(also suspiciously)* And besides, our hair had turned gray overnight and we'd nothing but aches and pains.

GRUBBINGRABBER: Of course, you did . . but lookee here, fellahs. It's cold and damp here, the dampness of the stream here and the cold were bound to get you feeling old and creaky sooner or later. Hair often goes gray overnight when you're suffering a bad time and failing to find treasure and eating a poor diet. It's all perfectly natural.

Now I ask you boys - could a man steal 40 years of your life, now I ask you . . ? Look, I've a great deal for you. I'll give you 300 down, that's 100 each - and just for the three quarters of the mine that the old professor didn't steal from you. And then I'll make out monthly paychecks for each of you every month for 40 years just for your work in my good, clean, healthy chemical factory down in the beautiful valley. Then I'll sell each of you a little house there for about 300 down payment each and the rest to be paid off monthly at only 3% interest over say roughly 20 years. I'll give you the details later.

Think of a calm, stressless life with no real hard toil . . just a little pushbutton factory job where you can sit all day long.

HANK: *(looking Grubbingrabber up and down, slowly)* Now when I think about it - you're very believable, you are real good. But no, I don't buy that, Georgie - not for one moment - nothing is as stressful and mean and ornery as working for someone else - sitting at a machine in a bad smelling factory. Oh, no thanks - I like to be my own boss. I don't want to be your pet poodle, Georgie.

HAL, HARRY, HANK: *(as they cringe and crawl and roll over and play dead and hold up one paw)* WOOF, WOOF, BOW WOW, HOWL, HOWL, YELP, YELP.

HAL: Me too. I'd rather have me for a boss than you. We trusted you once - just for a little while - and you slunk off - a thief in the night with our goods and gear.

HARRY: You'll never persuade me to work for a bossman - that's no such thing as a good job -

and as Hal says, why did you slink off the last time?

GRUBBINGRABBER: Look guys, I didn't steal anything from you.

HANK: How come the goods vanished with you when you ran off and then we felt old and tired?

GRUBBINGRABBER: Why, digging for treasures is bound to make you old and gray and tired. As for getting out of here, I had no choice. I ran off because the old professor chased me off. Yes that's it. He had a gun and he ordered me off so that he could steal you blind. It was all the work of Professor Luck - falsely so-called if you ask me.

***Professor Luck enters** from the forest shadows.*

PROFESSOR LUCK: *(entering)* O really Mr. Squaredeal. Then what happened to my gun - no one else saw it - did you, my partners? *(they shake their heads)*

And what did I do with the things you stole? Did I make them disappear or bury them to come back later and find them - hide them like treasure trove - a few utensils and tools? And why did you not shout out when I ordered you away? And why did I stay and give my new friends, 10,000 in advance. Your upfront payment is still only 300. Ha, ha, ha 300 down for the mine and your word. Only <u>your</u> word for all the rest and even then you want all the money they own, 9,000 or 10,000 - just for the down payments on houses.

GRUBBINGRABBER: *(haughtily)* My word, my good sir, is as good as gold.

HANK: Well, I'd prefer to dig for gold or silver or whatever we can find.

HAL: Even if it means I grow gray and old.

HARRY: I don't believe your story Mr. Squaredeal. How about giving us back our bits and pieces?

HANK: Not to mention giving us back our youth?

GRUBBINGRABBER: Give you back your youth? That's a freaky thing to say. Can't be done.

PROFESSOR: *(to three goldbugs)* That's true, the first honest thing he has told us - he can take - but he can't give. He can take your life but he can't give it back to you. Trust him if you wish. It's up to you.

The three bugs roll up their sleeves as though to tackle Mr. Squaredeal. He holds up his hands and backs away towards the nearby woods.

GRUBBINGRABBER: Now, please fellahs, take it easy. I was only offering you a fair meal deal, a fair offer of three good jobs. What's wrong with that. You can always turn me down. I don't mind. *(as they still advance towards him grimly)* Lookee here gentleman, bosses, captains, professors, I tell you what - I'll bring back the things I borrowed from you - all of them. *(to audience)* I only borrowed them didn't I?

AUDIENCE: Oh, no you didn't.

GRUBBINGRABBER: Oh yes I did.

AUDIENCE: Oh, no you didn't.

GRUBBINGRABBER: I didn't steal anything did I?

AUDIENCE: Oh, yes you did.

GRUBBINGRABBER: I'm not a liar or a thief, am I?

AUDIENCE: Oh yes you are.

GRUBBINGRABBER: Oh no I'm not.

AUDIENCE: *(slowly)* Oh - yes - you - are.

GRUBBINGRABBER: *(slowly)* No - no - no.

AUDIENCE: Boo, boo, boo.

The three treasure bugs continue to slowly advance towards Grubbingrabber as he turns and begins to run off-stage. He drops his axe and plunges into the creek, coming up soaked, scared and yelling.

GRUBBINGRABBER: See, I'll just go and get those things that I borrowed - I'll bring them back to you - real soon. Just let me go, fellahs.

Grubbingrabber runs off, dripping wet and terrified, into the woods, exiting right. The Professor and the three bugs all laugh and shake hands and clap each other on the back.

PROFESSOR: *(shaking his head)* You almost believed him but I admit he's a plausible rogue. He states his case well - I'll say that for him.

Curtain

SCENE THREE

The same scene as before. ***Enter the Professor,*** *carrying a walking stick, lit at the pointed end. It is late at night. The stage is dimly lit. The figure of the Professor is lightly spotlighted and dances around waving the walking stick like a wand.*

PROFESSOR: At last the mine is quiet and deserted. Now I can work my magic on these rocks and touch a golden gleam into these streams. *(he laughs)* Ha, ha, little did those old prospectors see through my disguise. Little did they realize that I am the one some call

Professor Luck, the Gold Bug King. Hee, hee. An old Professor, yes, *(shakes his head)* but Professor of Luck. Now what would an old ordinary professor be doing here in these remote hills, miles from good books but yet among the worms. *(hee, hee)* But no one has suspected me. *(he points his stick here and there)*

Here! Let silver crawl up from far beneath the bones of the earth. Let the silver lie just beneath the surface. *(he points his stick)* There - let silver streams swim up from the pools of health in the caves of ice. Yes, let the silver swim up into this silver stream from far beneath the green hills of the earth. O let the crystal grains appear and swim about like stars in the starry night.

The professor dashes about the stage pointing his lighted stick here and there.

This is the only way anyone ever found treasure - by good luck and hard work. Here and here is the luck. Tomorrow the old prospectors will find these crystal streams of healthy spring water. Suddenly they will be rewarded. *(he straightens up proudly)* I am the Gold Bug King, who worked my magic in these dreary diggings. Good luck to the digger, here and there.

A clear crystal jet stream of water shoots up out of the rock, near center stage.

Professor sings **GOLD BUGS**.

Professor Luck struts up and down with his coattails held behind his back, cane in hand, shaking it here and there. Professor Luck raises his arms wide in great self-pride, then shakes his cane in the air and smiles as he struts back and forth across the stage, then bows to audience. The three bugs waken up.

HAL: Just a minute now, Professor, what are you doing there with those lights?

HARRY: Is this a joke? What are you doing, Professor?

HANK: Is this a dream or are you somehow doing strange things?

PROFESSOR: Well, I did tell you my profession. I forgot to mention my full name. Professor Stargazer N. Luck. N for numbers.

I'm the one you summoned from the echo and the echo called me. Remember?

HAL: No. I don't believe it.

HARRY: You're him, for real?

HANK: *(sighing)* Well here we were, getting old and getting nowhere . . .

PROFESSOR: No one is going nowhere in *my* presence.

HANK: Then perhaps meeting you now has been worth the wait?

PROFESSOR: Yes, I'm Professor Luck - the man with all the destiny numbers and the magic pointer.

HAL: But you'll help us?

PROFESSOR: Yes, of course. I'm always willing to give *at least a little* help to the hardworking, the honest, the hopeful. You should have sent for me sooner.

The professor pokes his lightie-up stick at the three old goldbugs.

PROFESSOR: I can't bring back your stolen time but I can give you the luck of healthy and vigorous old bones. Here.

The professor's stick glows like a star and the three treasure bugs begin to dance around like three year-olds.

ALL THREE: Luck. Luck, Professor Luck has come at last.

And then the three treasure bugs begin to speak more slowly and soberly . . .

HAL: We've still lost our youth . . .

HARRY: Well, at least the torments and toils of youth are all gone away.

HANK: But strange and spooky things are happening.

The professor points his stick at some of the high rocks nearby and jumps around and dances and cries.

PROFESSOR: See the water jets - that's not gold but silver water. See, more silver water all sparkling - all you need to do is bottle it, label it and drink it and sell it. There's millions in silver mineral water all around you.

HANK: What, no gold?

HAL: Any kind of silver is a success. We'll take it, drink it and sell it. Everybody needs good healthy water.

HARRY: No diamonds, no rubies, no treasure trove? But health and wealth just the same. Superoo!

The three goldbugs dance around Professor Luck, in joy and song.

PROFESSOR: Only discernment and wisdom and straight thinking stand between you and a life of clear outsight and inmost understanding - drink the magic silvery juice and enjoy health and dancing and singing.

They all sing **SQUIRRELS**.

From the shadows, slowly, sneakily, enters Georgie S. Grubbingrabber.

He is dressed in a business suit, striped shirt, bright red tie, gray socks and black shining shoes. His hair is neatly trimmed and brushed. He is clean-shaven and carries a briefcase. There are pens in his top jacket pocket.

GRUBBINGRABBER: *(smiling)* Hi there pals! Remember me, your old pal – Squaredeal? Hee. Hee.

HANK: Oh yes, you're the crook who stole our youth, goods, chattels and money. Hi, Pal. *(with sarcasm)* Then, after your last visit, we found some of our machines broken.

GRUBBINGRABBER: Now boys, you know that stealing your youth is impossible - that's just a misunderstanding. You boys have spent too much time up in these here sunny hills and old machinery is always breaking down you know.

HARRY: *(edging closer to Grubbingrabber)* Oh sure - we're nuts - you didn't really rip us off.

HANK: Yes, we've all gone treasure-trove. *(he sticks his thumbs in his ears and wags fingers)*

HAL: *(sinisterly approaching Grubbingrabber)* Why, it's our esteemed associate, Georgie. It's dusty here. Let me brush your lapels, old chap.

GRUBBINGRABBER: *(relieved)* Phew yea. You got it right. You just all got old naturally and it sort of went to your heads. Lookee here. I have a great deal - call me Squaredeal - now that you have a business and all, maybe you will be worrying a little. Now you need security, peace of mind, guarantees against a rainy day. Have I got an insurance policy for you all. Low low payment per month and covers you against sickness, hospitalization, loss of business profits and in case of sudden death a large bonus goes to your next of kill - I mean kin. Bad things can happen - you need protection from them now that you're going into business.

HAL: *(edging closer to Grubbingrabber)* Always on the make, eh? But, for once, yes, I agree with you, Squaredeal.

GRUBBINGRABBER: *(eagerly)* Yes, it makes sense.

HAL: Sure it does. We all need guarantees of security - a good insurance policy against what could happen to anyone - like injury or hospitalization.

The three goldbugs have now surrounded Grubbingrabber.

HANK: *(calmly and pacifying)* Sure, Squaredeal. No doubt you have such a real good insurance policy to cover your own needs.

GRUBBINGRABBER: *(nervously)* Oh sure, boys - me and my loved ones are well covered for all risks.

HAL: Great, Georgie, old boy - then you won't mind us seizing you . . .

They seize Georgie and bind him to a tree.

Grubbingrabber begs for mercy.

GRUBBINGRABBER: Help. Let me go, this is kidnapping. *(to audience)* Call the mountain rangers. Tell them to let me go. *(to silent* *audience)* Well . . they're kidnappers, aren't they?

AUDIENCE: Oh no they're not.

GRUBBINGRABBER: Oh yes they are.

AUDIENCE: Oh no they're not.

HAL: You don't mind do you, us tying you up here.

HANK: And . . ah . . inflicting a few, well-insured against, injuries.

HARRY: Then leaving you here for the wild-dogs to perform their cute little tricks and hoop jumps and bow wow begs for you. We'll leave it to them - we don't want to become your poodles, your performing dogs. Let the wild dogs do that for you.

*Harry, Hal and Hank each act out their role in the following song - **WHAT A GOOD DOG**.*

WHAT A GOOD DOG

Sung: Cheerful and Rollicking

VERSE ONE

d r m m m - m r d m s s - s
Now the bad dogs today just won't do as we say
l s m d - d r m l_1
But still they expect to get food
d m m m - m r d m s s - s
Why should they get fed and why should they get bed
l - l s m d r m - r d
When their manners are not very good.

REFRAIN:

m - m s s s s l t d^1 - d^1 l - d^1
I will sit up and beg and then hold up a leg
l s m d - d r m - l_1 m l_1
I'll stick out my tongue and agree (you'll see)
d m m m m r d m s s s
O please let me do all you're asking me to
l s m d r m r d r d
O what a good dog I will be (you'll see)

HARRY *(singing)*

I'll go round in a loop or I'll jump through a hoop
I'll crawl on the ground and lie low
(Harry crawls and rolls over and covers his eye with his hands)
I'll cover my face and pretend to say Yes
I'll bring back whatever you throw

HAL *(singing)*

It is quite an affront if you can't do a stunt
Like cringe away down and play dead
(Hal cringes as though dead, then lies possum)
If you can't earn your pay in some groveling way
I don't think you ought to get paid

HANK *(singing)*

I will sit up and beg and then hold up a leg
I'll stick out my tongue and agree *(you'll see)*
(Hank puts out his tongue and nods)
O please let me do all you're asking me to
O what a good dog I will be *(you'll see)*
(Hank holds his hands before him like begging paws)

GRUBBINGRABBER: *(to audience)* They've no right to treat me like this. I'm not a liar, a cheat and a thief, am I?

AUDIENCE: Oh yes you are.

GRUBBINGRABBER: Oh no I'm not.

AUDIENCE: *(slowly)* Oh - yes - you - are.

GRUBBINGRABBER: I'm innocent of all crimes. Oh yes I am.

AUDIENCE: Oh no you're not.

GRUBBINGRABBER: I never did any harm did I?

AUDIENCE: Oh yes you did.

GRUBBINGRABBER: Oh no I didn't.

AUDIENCE: Oh yes you did.

GRUBBINGRABBER: What do you take me for?

AUDIENCE: Boo, boo, boo.

Grubbingrabber is still tied to the tree. The three goldbugs pretend to be dogs and bow wow and bark and jump and beg as they join hand in hand with the professor and all dance around the tree.

Grubbingrabber, still bound, begs for mercy, wailing and howling, twisting and turning. There is a roll of thunder, lights go out and suddenly the Squaredealer is struck by lightning, yells in pain, struggles free from the tree and escapes toward the forest, shaking his fist and shouting as he limps away.

GRUBBINGRABBER: I'll get you all one day. No one ever escapes me - I'm the boss. See? So you want to be your own boss, do you, eh? Then ha, ha, I'm telling you I'll get you.

Exit Grubbingrabber.

They all sing again ***GOLDBUGS, SQUIRRELS and WHAT A GOOD DOG.*** *Then they all dance around the fire and Hopeful Hal points to the flames.*

HAL: See in the flames the faces of old friends filled with love and laughing and the faces of former foes frowning and cast down with disappointment.

HARRY: See up there the sun struggles free from his nightchains, drags his face up out of the far hills.

HANK: And hear the high blue dawnbird beginning the new day by singing a new song that no one has ever heard before.

Then the tall professor slowly slips among the trees, waving his magic stick to the goldbugs.

PROFESSOR: I must travel on. I hear someone else trying and crying for me out there.

Then Professor Luck disappears into the shortening shadows of the daybreak that creeps slowly up upon the old mine camp and the fountains of clear spring water.

HANK: Where has Professor Luck gone?

HAL: Out there into the great winds and forests and rivers and seas.

HARRY: *(looking far into the distance)* Yes, and there he will travel for evermore, wandering at his will with his magic stick and destiny numbers, alive and willing to help those who have courage and goodness and faith, somewhere out there far along the little known and lonesome trails of the mind.

Curtain

END OF PLAYSCRIPT

THE INTERNATIONAL CONVENTION OF BURGLARS

A Short Story and a One-Act Play

The Story

All the acrimony and the argument began in a large meeting hall on the occasion of the Annual Convention of the International Brotherhood of Burglars. Along the inside back of the hall was the banner "International Brotherhood of Burglars" and the date of the current year. In front of this banner and below it was a platform running from right to left. On the platform stood a long table with several chairs facing the audience. Steps lead up to the platform at each side.

In front of the platform was a wide aisle, flanked on either side by single chairs and benches facing the platform, with a space between the platform and the front seats. On either side were pillars, windows and signs saying 'Exit', 'No Smoking', 'Ladies and Gents Restrooms'.

The hall was well lit throughout with particular focus on the center areas. There were loud murmurs and shouts from the audience as the convention members made their way to the platform or to the chairs in front of the platform.

Among the leaders were the Chairman of the Meeting and Brotherhood – Burglar Billy, followed by the General Secretary - Sammy Secrets, the Mayor of Sillihead - Old Jellybelly, Alderman Fatso and Alderman Freako.

All strutted along the platform, pompously puffed up with a sense of their own importance, waving and finger wagging and bowing stiltedly to their union members and townspeople who also filed in to take their places in the vacant seats of the meeting hall.

However, these latter union members and townsfolk were not getting along well. They were arguing and pushing, pointing fingers, shaking fists and threatening each other, both within the ranks of the two groups and between the two groups (unionists and public).

The burglars and the townspeople were mixed together as they entered but after much pushing and shoving they re-ranked into two distinct groups - burglars on the left side of the aisle and townspeople on the right side of the aisle. They continued to jostle each other, fight over chairs, elbow each other and act in an unruly way.

Burglars were dressed in convict style in black pants and shoes, black and white striped T shirts, black berets, close shaven, clean necked. They wore dark glasses and carried on their belts such gear as coshes, jimmies, crowbars, flash lights or similar.

The townspeople were wearing somewhat old fashioned clothes, including hats and handbags or purses. They appeared slightly whacky, eccentric or yokelly because of their weird gestures, scratching of heads vacantly or staring into space.

The burglar officials sat on the left side of the platform with the chairman in the center and the mayor and aldermen to the right. They too were dressed as their followers except that the chairman burglar carried a gavel and wore a jacket whereas the mayor wore a ceremonial robe and a wide floral chain of office. The platform party sat in various stages of disarray and confusion except for the chairman who banged his gavel on the table and called for order.

The chairman, Burglar Billy, cried out, "Order! Order!" and pointed to his audience. "Hey, you there, stop slaughtering each other. Order! Calm down, good folks. Order!"

As the rest of the platform party smiled and waved and tittered at their audience, everyone calmed down somewhat.

The chairman Burglar Billy, rather stiltedly announced, "This is an auspicious occasion in the history of the Burglars' Union. Here we are in the fine city of Sillihead - one of the nation's premier seaside resorts. On my left here, the mayor of the city wishes to make a .. short . . ."

Burglar Billy was interrupted by the entrance of a wandering bugler carrying a bugle slung over his right shoulder. He was dressed as a member of the British Indian Armed Forces. The bugler took up a position at the head of the aisle facing the seated attendees, with his back to the platform, to the consternation of the platform party who motioned him to get out of the way.

The mayor waved at the bugler, "You down there, clear the decks!"

The bugler took off his bugle and raised it into the air near his face. He announced somewhat keenly, "My beloved fellow buglers." He peered at them sharply, "Ah, you're in mufti, I see, in civilian dress - well I did not know – didn't have time to change. I just saw the banner sign outside." He peered around, puzzled, "What! No bugles here? Oh good, let me start off the meeting with *reveille*."

He began to toot on his horn as the others generally tore their hair and covered their ears.

The general secretary stood up and began to scream, "Stop. This is the Burglars Union, burglars, burglars, can't you read? It's not buglers, it's burglars."

The bugler began to laugh and cried out, "Ha, ha, burglars - how silly – there's no such thing as a burglars' union." Then he read the banner again carefully, "No, it must mean buglers - here I'm the genuine Bugler Boy Bingham of the Old 52nd - the perennial annuals they called us - get it - 52 weeks in the . . ."

A burglar from the audience interrupted him, taking him by the scruff of the neck, to cries of "out with him" and "dump him out."

The mayor gritted his teeth and muttered, "Can't you spell burglar, Burglar, Burglar. B-U-R-G-L-A-R?"

The bugler struggled and cried out, "But it must be a misprint for bugler – there's no such thing as a burglars' convention. Hey stop." They all paused and fell silent for a moment but the bugler continued, undeterred. "It must be a mistake - it must read Buglers. I know what it is, I know, you're all amateur buglers and you don't want a professional to show you up - to embarrass you. I understand - but you need to hear a real bugler once in a while, Listen . . ."

He blew another call on his horn as shouting and turmoil returned. They threw him out, still protesting. The others now relaxed and the platform party reverted to its smiling, waving and tittering. The seated attendees relaxed smugly, pleased with the expulsion of the bugler and smiled at each other, dusted their hands together and nodded to one another as much as to say "good riddance to bad rubbish."

The chairman stood up once again, "I am Burglar Billy, Chair of the Burglars' Union. I thank you ladies and gentlemen for coming to order. And now, it gives me great pleasure to call upon the Mayor of the City of Sillihead, Old Jellybelly, to lead the meeting." He bowed his head respectfully, "Mayor Jellybelly, the platform is yours, Sir."

The mayor rose arrogantly, twitching and shaking as he addressed the meeting. He began formally, "On behalf of the citizens of Sillihead, Alderman Fatso." Fatso stood up and nodded. "And Alderman Freako." Freako raised up his hands above his head, champion style, grinned foolishly and then sat down. "I would like to welcome the Burglar's Union to their 97th Annual Convention and the first to be held outside prison walls. This is also our first city convention for 20 years and let us hope that it encourages other major national groups to come here, in future.

"While the Burglars' Union are here we need to improve relations between our ordinary citizens and these former burglars who so much need our understanding and help in rehabilitation. To this end I have arranged for a series of friendly sociological lectures on the relationship between burglars and householders - to help make friends between the two sides."

A few boos and hisses came from the townspeople.

Chairman Billy Burglar looked embarrassed but the mayor continued stubbornly. "We will now hear the inaugural lecture from the Burglars' Union Social Worker who will give her brief talk on G.A.R.P. - Generally Accepted Rehabilitation Principles."

At this point there was weak applause in an eccentric way - with gasps, tongues out, fingers in mouth, blank looks, strange stares, head-scratching zombie-like stiffness, open mouths, fearful twitching, shaking and trembling. Suddenly, the bugler banged on his drum and tooted on his horn.

Everyone then sat down except the Union Social Worker who arranged her notes, stood up and began to address the assembly, smiling and bowing to very weak applause.

She began nervously, "It gives me such great pleasure to be asked to build up the good relations between the burglars and the townsfolk. We really need to understand each other - for, at times in the past, we have failed to support and help and cherish our friend to friend relationship."

The burglars cheered but the townsfolk looked sick, stared at each other in surprise and generally disapproved of these remarks, pointing incredulously at the burglars and shaking their heads in blank astonishment.

One of the townsfolk stood up and cried out in surprise, "Our friends? You gotta be kidding. Friends? Oh yeah. I thought they were supposed to be tourists and visitors bringing money in and then getting out!"

At this, one of the burglars spoke up in unbelief, "So? We should spend our money here and then get out. That's nice. Is that what tourism is all about? Oh yeah? I thought anyone of us would be welcome to holiday here. Can we buy a home and relax or retire here or not? How about a little two-way give and take? Then, after we give a little and then take a little, then and only then do we get out. How about a win win situation? How's about a tit for tat eh?"

The burglars began to erupt and yell in support. However, they all calmed down as the chairman tapped his gavel on the table and shouted, "Order, order. This whole meeting is an exercise in community relations."

The social worker appeared to be relieved and smiled at being able to resume, "Look here, my fellow townspeople - I realize that we all have an irrational fear of burglars but let us realize that these fears are unrealistic. We fear the unknown."

At this point the townspeople looked at each other in disgust and pointed thumbs sarcastically at the speaker.

One of the townsmen cried out, "Hey, we know burglars only too well. It's what we know about them that makes us nervous. It's simple - it's as simple as this. They want to steal. Rip us off, O.K?"

The townsfolk began to cheer.

The social worker continued primly, "Yes, I realize that you'll have an irrational fear of burglars but I ask you, Sir, have you personally ever been burgled?"

One of the townsmen replied, "Yes, twice."

The social worker inquired, "And what age are you Sir?"

The townsman replied, "Eighty."

The social worker was delighted, "See what I mean? On average you've been burgled only once every 40 years. Is that really so bad? Look, we need to minimize burglary. We can never do away with it completely. How can we minimize it? By rehabilitating burglars. See? That's why we need to follow G.A.R.P."

The burglars cheered.

The townsfolk looked confused and one of them asked, "What's G.A.R.P?"

The social worker sighed and replied wearily, "G.A.R.P. is Generally Accepted Rehabilitation Principles."

The burglars smiled approvingly as the townsfolk looked confused and doubtful.

A townswoman was still not clear, "Spell it out more. What exactly are these principles?"

The social worker replied, "Let me read them to you. And remember, these principles are approved by Government and Big Business as well as by the Burglars' Union. Number One: All doors must contain glass or be placed beside glass panels."

A reporter stood up angrily and demanded to know, "Why? Why glass panels on doors? It doesn't make sense to me. Do you mean to say that you want this just to make things easy for these burglars?"

The chairman replied testily, "Please sit down. Don't interrupt. Hear out our explanation of G.A.R.P. and then we will be open for comments."

The reporter replied, somewhat reluctantly, "Oh, very well! But your explanation better be good!"

The social worker sweetly replied, "Thank you, Mr. Reporter. Now - to our principles again. Number Two: No crocodiles, bad dogs or broken glass around the house."

The chairman burglar seemed to be as pleased as punch and perked up, "Hear, hear, if anyone's going to break glass around the house, it's going to be us, eh, fellahs?"

At this point there were cheers from burglars on the floor but loud boos from the townsfolk.

The social worker continued, "Number Three: No guns, baseball or cricket bats, knives or catapults to be kept in houses. Anyone who injures a burglar in the course of his unlawful occupation of burglary shall be guilty of a criminal offence - the offense of self-defense - totally unacceptable in all paternalistic police states."

Again this was greeted with both boos and cheers.

But the social worker plodded on, "Number Four: Burglars' Union to support lawyers who will bring civil lawsuits against dangerous self-defenders and vigilantes."

Alderman Freako drew a large knife out of his sleeve and chuckled, "Oh, I think that's going too far. We have to be able to defend ourselves."

More boos and cheers from the floor.

The social worker was not to be stopped in her verbal train journey. "Just a minute - Number Five of our G.A.R.P. is that we should respect the right of all burglars to earn a living and feed their families. Families, families, yes, yes, yes, families. Doesn't that clinch the argument. They must support their families. Otherwise, burglars will have to take to crimes . . ."

Alderman Fatso interrupted, "But burglary is a crime . . ."

The social worker triumphantly interrupted, "Please let me finish! I was going to say." She paused intently for a long breath, before she continued. "If burglars cannot feed their families, they will take to crimes much worse than mere stealing - such as violent robbery, robbery with murder. Crimes of smuggling, slashing, terrorism, extortion, blackmail and so on. Therefore, we must at least give them a fair chance to carry out their relatively harmless burglaries."

She raised her voice above the boos and jeers and the hoorays and cheers.

"In fact, G.A.R.P. Number Six says that householders should always leave lying about - a decent sum of money in cash - so as to give any stray burglar an incentive to get out of your home real quick. Otherwise he might set fire to it or even wreck it in disgust."

The same townswoman began to harangue the nearest burglars on the stage, "Oh, so you'll burn down my house will you?" She lifted up an umbrella threateningly and strode over to the burglar's side. "Burn me out if I don't give you protection money will you?"

The chairman burglar was absolutely outraged, "Ma'am," he shouted, "that's a misrepresentation of what was said. Nobody wants to burn your house. All you do is leave some money around your house just in case a burglar needs it for his family."

There were more boos and cheers as the two sides began to roll up their sleeves and showed signs of coming to blows.

Finally, the chairman tried to calm things down. "Please, please," he was pleading and almost weeping as he begged one and all, "let's have a brief intermission so that we can discuss all this in peace and quiet and come to an honest agreement between us. After all, we're bringing money into the town now by holding this convention here. So there are two sides to every debate. Money is money and money talks and who cares where the money comes from so long as we get it. O.K?"

But the townsfolk continued to protest and the chairman summed up. "Look, we've heard the Burglars' Union Social Worker. After we all calm down and have a nice break we'll hear what the townsfolk have to say. We'll hear both sides before we set up a policy document. All right. Is that fair?"

The two sides calmed down somewhat but were still arguing with each other as they milled around and took a short break.

A little while later the burglars and townsfolk filed back into their seats but this time they were shaking fists at each other as well as walking sticks and umbrellas and coshes and jimmies and flashlights.

In high spirits, the chairman burglar spoke up, "Calm down now. I promised that the townsfolk would have a chance to make their case. And yes, I'm a man of my word. Mayor Jellybelly, it's your turn now to comment on our proposed policy based on G.A.R.P. You did approve the plan before this meeting, right?"

The mayor nodded, "Well, when I heard about Generally Accepted Rehabilitation Principles, I thought that rehabilitation meant putting rogues back into life after prison and putting honest reformed thieves out to hard graft and work like the rest of us - that was my mistake, of course. I know now that modern rehabilitation means keeping them out of prison at all costs. Now that's all right only so long as they go out and earn an honest living."

At this, one of the burglars cried out in agony, "But my resume is so bad, how can I get a job? My phony life upsets even me and I wrote it!"

The mayor was astonished, "If reading over your resume doesn't make you feel great - you're just not a good enough liar and whose fault is that?"

The same burglar replied, "I cannot tell a lie. I confess freely it wasn't me - it was him over there."

This exasperated the mayor. He banged his fist into his other hand and screamed, "Shut up. Shut up. Shut up."

At this performance, the townsfolk cheered loudly.

The secretary of the Burglars Union was not at all satisfied at this outburst and began to moan. "But surely you understand Mayor, people will not give us jobs and we still have to feed our families."

The mayor replied testily, "Well, there's jobs that don't need honesty - like digging power-line trenches."

He paused as howls of anger rose from the burglars. "Or flying an airplane or being a politician."

Now there were subdued growls from some of the burglars as the mayor continued.

"Or TV evangelist or media moron but the point is sometimes it's a toss-up whether we stop you from feeding your families or whether you stop us from feeding ours - by ripping us off. So we just have to find reasonable compromises.

"I propose therefore that the six Generally Accepted Rehabilitation Principles should be rejected by the meeting as being too one-sided in favor of burglars. Let us have a minute for discussion and then we'll vote on it and whichever side wins the vote - that decision will be officially accepted by the convention meeting. All right?"

The mayor raised his hands and smiled benevolently as everyone nodded. "Good, good." He pronounced. "No hard feelings. No crude yelling or shouting or insulting."

Everyone somewhat reluctantly but sincerely nodded in agreement.

Everyone brightened and relaxed and agreed as the mayor concluded. "No arguments. Just an orderly, democratic, intelligent vote, straight up or down, to accept G.A.R.P. or not, O.K?

"Make your decision known. Yes or No on these slips of paper. It's either - Make life easy for burglars "YES" to avoid worse crises or "NO" do not, O.K.?"

At this, most people smiled and agreed as the mayor looked very pleased with himself. "Let's just pass out the voting slips then. I'm a fervent believer in democracy myself . . democracy . . ."

While the voting slips were being passed out, the bugler reappeared, dressed as before with bugle in hand, between the burglars and the townsfolk.

The bugler then began his prepared homily on democracy, "Democracy, yes, yes, truly so. Buglers of the World at this great Annual Convention. I am a true member of your union. It cannot possibly be burglars - that is clearly a typo, a mere technical printing error, in short, a mistake - in fact rubbish. It is all a great misrepresentation. I am a truly professional bugler and should be admitted. You must hear what I can do with this old bugle, then you will want to admit me in the name of true democracy. Listen to my proof of full eligibility for membership. Listen, I truly represent the working classes at the level of skilled labor.

"Remember this, the International of all the Buglers has a duty to represent every properly apprenticed and journeyman bugler in order to protect his skills from exploitation by big biz, big gubmint or big gunz and in order to prevent his loss of livelihood due to untrained and unlicensed scab labor."

He paused, began to think hard and then shrugged before continuing, "The class struggle can only be won if all and sundry truly qualified, apprenticed labor are permitted to join the union. I have no objection to paying the full union dues commensurate with my earning capacity which is nil anyway. Furthermore, comrades, I am one of those who call to arms the sons and daughters of the proletarian revolution to overthrow, by workingman solidarity, the despicable capitalist despots of the western world. Listen . . . Listen comrades. . ."

His hearers were stunned and confused as the bugler played a cavalry charge on his horn. Finally, chaos broke out and both sides attacked each other vigorously, using all available weapons.

Desperately, the bugler tried to overrule the violence, "Stop, listen, do not kill each other on account of poor me. Hear what I can do."

Somehow, for no apparent reason, a total melee took place as the bugle calls and the fighting persisted.

The bugler continued bugling a charge as both sides attacked each other.

Finally he shouted, "G.A.R.P. for ever! G.A.R.P. is GARBAGE."

END OF STORY

The Playscript

OUTLINE OF THE PLAY
SCENE ONE: Community Needs
SCENE TWO: Family Values
SCENE THREE: Workingman Solidarity
Music: Four songs: *Seaside Town; Boom, Boom, Boom; Gold Bugs; Drink Your Tea*
Stage Time: Approximately 30 minutes
Age Group: All Ages
Set: The same for all scenes

CHARACTERS IN THE PLAY
CHAIRMAN OF THE INTERNATIONAL BROTHERHOOD OF BURGLARS - Burglar Billy
GENERAL SECRETARY – Sammy Secrets
NEWS REPORTER
A BUGLER - who has lost his way
(he should preferably be an East Indian who may be dressed in cloth cap and workingman's clothes or for more comic effect as a sepoy in old British Raj)
MAYOR OF SILLIHEAD - Old Jellybelly welcoming the convention. He carries and bangs a large drum.
TWO ALDERMEN - Fatso and Freako also on the welcome committee
A SOCIAL WORKER, speaking on behalf of the union
SEVEN ACTORS and four to twenty extras as burglars or townspeople in attendance. All seven parts may be

played by male or female actors as there is little gender definition in the skit.

Scene One - Community Needs

The scene is a large meeting hall on the occasion of the Annual Convention of the International Brotherhood of Burglars. Downstage, along the backdrop facing the audience, clear of head level is the banner "International Brotherhood of Burglars" and the date of the current year. In front of this banner and below it is a platform running almost from right to left-stage holding a long table with several chairs facing the audience. Steps lead up to the platform at each side.

Center-stage, from the platform to front-stage is a wide aisle, flanked on either side by single chairs or benches facing the platform, with a space for action and movement between the platform and the front seats.

Right and left-stage are pillars, windows, signs saying 'Exit' or 'No Smoking' or 'Ladies' or 'Gents' or 'Restrooms', etc., and minor variations of this scene which are a matter for artistic judgment. The impression is that of looking at a meeting hall from the entrance to the platform.

The stage is well lit throughout with particular focus on the center-stage areas. There are loud murmurs and shouts from offstage as the convention members make their way to either the platform or to the chairs in front of the platform.

Enter from right the Chairman of the Meeting and Brotherhood – Burglar Billy, followed by the General Secretary - Sammy Secrets, the Mayor of Sillihead - Old Jellybelly, Alderman Fatso and Alderman Freako.

All file along the platform, pompously puffed up with a sense of their own importance, waving and finger wagging and bowing stiltedly to their union members and townspeople who also file in to take their places in the vacant seats of the stage meeting hall.

However, these latter union members and townsfolk are not getting along well. They are arguing and pushing, pointing fingers, shaking fists and threatening each other, both within the ranks of the two groups and between the two groups (unionists and public).

The burglars and the townspeople are mixed together as they enter but after much pushing and shoving they re-rank into two distinct groups - burglars on the left side of the aisle and townspeople on the right side of the aisle. They continue to jostle each other, fight over chairs, elbow each other and act in an unruly way.

Burglars are dressed convict style in black pants and shoes, black and white striped T shirts, black berets, close shaven, clean necked. They wear dark glasses and carry on their belts such gear as coshes, jimmies, crowbars, flash lights or similar. The townspeople are wearing somewhat old-fashioned clothes, including hats and handbags or purses. They should appear slightly whacky or eccentric or yokelly by such means as heavy, strange makeup, weird gestures, scratching head vacantly, staring into space and so on.

Similarly, the burglar officials sit on the left side of the platform with the chairman in the center and the mayor and aldermen to the right. They too are dressed as their followers except that the chairman burglar carries a gavel and wears a jacket whereas the mayor wears a ceremonial robe and a wide floral chain of office. The platform party sit in various stages of disarray and confusion except for the chairman who bangs his gavel on the table and calls for order.

CHAIRMAN BURGLAR BILLY: Order! Order! *(pointing to his audience)* Hey you there, stop slaughtering each other. Order! Calm down, good folks. Order!

As rest of the platform party smile and wave and titter at their audience, everyone calms down somewhat.

CHAIRMAN BURGLAR BILLY: *(pompously)* This is an auspicious occasion in the history of the Burglars' Union. Here we are in the fine city of Sillihead one of the nation's premier seaside resorts. On my left here the mayor of the city wishes to make a . . short . . .

Mayor leads company in singing:

SEASIDE TOWN*

Sung: Jolly

VERSE 1:

d d f s l - s - f
Y'all come down to Seaside Town
f - s f r d
Seaside by the Sea
d l_1 d f l - l s f
Along the strand and over the sand
f s f m f s
Is all the fun you need
d l_1 - d r - *f* f s l - l s *f*
Some love to go to the slopes of snow
f - f - s - f r d
Seems kind of cold to me
r - d - r - m - *f* s l s *f*
But boats are afloat with friendly folk
f - s - r m d *f*
In Seaside by the Sea

VERSE 1:
Y'all come down to Seaside Town
Seaside by the Sea
Along the strand and over the sand
Is all the fun you need
Some love to go to the slopes of snow
Seems kind of cold to me *(shivers)*
But boats are afloat with friendly folk
In Seaside by the Sea.

REFRAIN:
d l_1 - d r - *f* f s l - l s *f*
So skid in the snow, or climb high or low
d l_1 - d r - *f* f s l - l s *f*
Let the big city lights bring you flutters and frights
f - f - s - f r - r d
Fly south till you catch a flee
r - r - d - r - m - *f* s l s *f*
But that's not the way we pass the day
r - r - d - r - m - *f* s l s *f*
And that's not quite how we spend the night
f - s - r m d *f*
In Seaside by the Sea

REFRAIN:
So skid in the snow, climb high or low
Let the big city lights bring you flutters and frights
Fly south till you catch a flee
But that's not the way pass the day
And that's not quite how we spend the night
In Seaside by the Sea.

VERSE 2:
There are sights and sounds and tastes abound
In the mists of memory
The soft ice-cream is a beautiful dream
There's a nice old pot of hot tea
And there is no gloom in the oyster room
It's all cockles and mussels for me
Or smack your lips on the fish and chips
In Seaside by the Sea.

VERSE 3:
O we used to float on a wobbly boat
And paddle and dive and cry
O the old ship's bell and the salty smell
Of the seaweeds a-swirling by
But there's a place where the good old days
Are still alive to me
It's down along with my pals and gals
Down beside the old seaside
In Seaside-by-the-Sea.

Burglar Billy is interrupted by the entrance from left-stage, between the platform and the audience, of a wandering bugler carrying a bugle slung over his right shoulder and dressed as a member of the British Indian Armed Forces. Bugler takes up a position at the head of the aisle facing the seated attendees, with his back to the platform, to the consternation of the platform party who motion him to get out of the way.

MAYOR: *(waving)* You down there, clear the decks!

BUGLER: *(taking off his bugle and raising it in the air, near his face)* My beloved fellow buglers *(peers at them)* Ah, you're in mufti, I see, in civilian dress - well I did not know – didn't have time to change. I just saw the banner sign outside. *(peers around)* What! No bugles here? Oh good, let me start off the meeting with "reveille."

He begins to toot on his horn as the others generally tear their hair and cover their ears.

GENERAL SECRETARY: *(standing up and screaming)* Stop. This is the burglars union, burglars, burglars. Can't you read? It's not buglers, it's burglars.

BUGLER: *(laughing)* Ha, ha, burglars - how silly. There's no such thing as a burglars' union. *(reads the banner)* No, it must mean buglers – here I'm the genuine Bugler Boy

Bingham of the Old 52nd. The perennial annuals they called us. Get it - 52 weeks in the . . .

A burglar from the audience interrupts him, taking him by the scruff of the neck, to cries of "out with him" and "dump him out."

MAYOR: Can't you spell burglar, Burglar, Burglar. B-U-R-G-L-A-R?

BUGLER: *(struggling)* But it must be a misprint for bugler – there's no such thing as a burglars' convention. HEY STOP. *(they all pause and fall silent for a moment)* It must be a mistake - it must read BUGLERS. I know what it is, I know, you're all amateur buglers and you don't want a professional to show you up - to embarrass you. I understand - but you need to hear a real bugler once in a while, LISTEN . . .

He blows another call on his horn as shouting and action returns. They throw him out, still protesting. The platform party relax and revert to its smiling, waving and tittering. The seated attendees relax and smile at each other smugly. Pleased with the expulsion of the bugler, they dust their hands together and

The International Convention of Burglars nod to one another as much as to say "good riddance to bad rubbish."

CHAIRMAN BURGLAR BILLY: *(resuming)* I am Burglar Billy, Chair of the Burglars' Union. I thank you ladies and gentlemen *(quietly)* for coming to order. And now, it gives me great pleasure to call upon the Mayor of the City of Sillihead, Old Jellybelly, to lead the meeting. *(respectfully)* Mayor Jellybelly, the platform is yours, Sir.

The mayor rises pompously, twitching and shaking.

MAYOR: On behalf of the citizens of Sillihead, Alderman Fatso *(Fatso stands up and nods)* and Alderman Freako *(Freako raises up his hands above his head, champion style, grins foolishly and sits down),* I would like to welcome the Burglar's Union to their 97th Annual Convention and the first to be held outside prison walls. This is also our first city convention for 20 years and let us hope that it encourages other major national groups to come here, in future.

While the Burglars' Union are here, we need to improve relations between our ordinary citizens and these former burglars who so much need our understanding and help in rehabilitation. To this end I have arranged for a series of friendly sociological lectures on the relationship between burglars and house-holders - to help make friends between the two sides.

A few boos and hisses from the townspeople. Chairman Burglar Billy looks embarrassed but the mayor continues stubbornly.

Anyhow, after a short break for refreshments we will hear the inaugural lecture from the Burglars' Union Social Worker who will give her brief talk on G.A.R.P. - Generally Accepted Rehabilitation Principles.

Weak applause in an eccentric way with gasps, tongues out, fingers in mouth, blank looks, strange stares, head-scratching zombie-like stiffness, open mouths, fearful twitching, shaking and trembling and so on.

Bugler bangs on his drum and toots on his horn. All sing: **BOOM, BOOM, BOOM.**

BOOM, BOOM, BOOM

Sung: Boisterous and Cheerful

VERSE 1:

d r f - f d
With a boom, boom, boom
d - r f - f - f - f d
We'll liven up and soon
d r maw - d - maw - d taw_1 s_1 - s_1 taw_1
We'll be rumbling and bumbling, like the
d taw_1 - d
Boom of doom
d r f f - s law
It's the Old Seaside noise
f maw d t_1 l_1 s_1
That brings the girls and boys
l_1 t_1 d t_1 l_1 m
To the brass band with all
r d t_1 l_1 t_1 l_1
The best in boom, boom, boom
l_1 - t_1 d - t_1 l_1 m - r d t_1 l_1 t_1 l_1
We'll follow the leader with the best in boom

VERSE 1:

With a boom, boom, boom
We'll liven up and soon
We'll be rumbling and bumbling
Like the boom of doom
It's the Old Seaside noise
That brings the girls and boys
To the brass band with all
The best in boom, boom, boom
We'll follow the leader with the best in boom.

VERSE 2:
When the grand brass band
Goes strutting up the strand
When the trombones go trum
To the sliding of the hand
Then the big brass drum
Goes a rum, a rum, a rum
It's the brass band for all
The best in boom, boom, boom
We'll follow the leader with the best in boom.

VERSE 3:
It's a toot, toot, toot
On the picky little flute
And a vroom, vroom, groan
On the long trombone
And a great drum blatter
That would make the seawaves scatter
It's the brass band with all
The best in boom, boom, boom
We'll follow the leader with the best in boom.

All follow the band off stage left.

Curtain

SCENE TWO - FAMILY VALUES

The same scene as before, with the same characters filing back into the same places after a short break. All sit down except the Union Social Worker who arranges her notes, stands up and begins to address the assembly, smiling and bowing to very weak applause.

SOCIAL WORKER: It gives me such great pleasure to be asked to build up the good relations between the burglars and the townsfolk. We really need to understand each other. For, at times in the past, we have failed to support and help and cherish our friend to friend relationship.

> *Burglars cheer but townsfolk look sick, stare at each other in surprise and generally disapprove of these remarks, pointing incredulously at the burglars and shaking their heads in blank astonishment.*

TOWNSFOLK: *(individual, one at a time)* Our friends? You gotta be kidding. Friends? Oh yeah. I thought they were supposed to be tourists and visitors bringing money in and then getting out!

BURGLARS: *(individual speakers, one at a time)* So - we should spend our money here then get out. That's nice. Is that what tourism is all about? Oh yeah? I thought anyone of us would be welcome to retire here. Can we buy a home and relax or retire here or not? How about a little two way give and take? Then, after we give a little and then take a little, then and only then do we get out. How about a win win situation? How's about a tit for tat eh?

Burglars erupt and yell in support. All calm down as the chairman taps his gavel on the table.

CHAIRMAN: Order, order. This whole meeting is an exercise in community relations.

SOCIAL WORKER: *(relieved and smiling at being able to resume)* Look here my fellow townspeople, I realize that we all have an irrational fear of burglars but let us realize that these fears are unrealistic. We fear the unknown.

Townspeople look at each other in disgust and point thumbs sarcastically at the speaker.

TOWNSMAN: Hey, we know burglars only too well. It's what we know about them that makes us nervous. It's simple - it's as simple as this. They want to steal. *(cheers from townsfolk)* Rip us off, O.K?

SOCIAL WORKER: Yes, I realize that you'll have an irrational fear of burglars but I ask you, Sir, have you personally ever been burgled?

TOWNSMAN: Yes, twice.

SOCIAL WORKER: And what age are you now, Sir?

TOWNSMAN: Eighty.

SOCIAL WORKER: See what I mean? On average you've been burgled only twice every 40 years. Is that really so bad? Look, we need to minimize burglary. We can never do away with it completely. How can we minimize it?

By rehabilitating burglars. See? That's why we need to follow G.A.R.P.

Burglars cheer. Townsfolk look confused.

TOWNSMAN: What's GARP?

SOCIAL WORKER: G.A.R.P. is Generally Accepted Rehabilitation Principles.

Burglars smile approvingly - townsfolk look confused and doubtful.

TOWNSWOMAN: Spell it out more. What exactly are these principles?

SOCIAL WORKER: Let me read them to you. And remember, these are approved by Government and Big Business as well as by the Burglars' Union.
1 All doors must contain glass or be placed beside glass panels.

REPORTER: *(standing up angrily)* Why? Why glass panels on doors? It doesn't make sense to me. Do you mean to say that you want this just to make things easy for these burglars?

CHAIRMAN: Please sit down. Don't interrupt. Hear out our explanation of G.A.R.P. and then we will be open for comments.

REPORTER: *(reluctantly)* Oh, very well! But your explanation better be good!

SOCIAL WORKER: *(sweetly)* Thank you, Mr. *(or Ms)* Reporter. Now to our principles again.
2 No crocodiles, bad dogs or broken glass around the house.

CHAIRMAN BURGLAR: Hear! Hear! If anyone's going to break glass around the house, it's going to be us, eh, fellahs?

Cheers from burglars on the floor - boos from the townsfolk.

SOCIAL WORKER:
3 No guns, baseball or cricket bats, knives or catapults to be kept in houses. Anyone who injures a burglar in the course of his unlawful occupation of burglary shall be guilty of a criminal offence - the offense of self-defense - totally unacceptable in all paternalistic police states.

Boos and cheers.

4 Burglars' Union to support lawyers who will bring civil lawsuits against dangerous self-defenders and vigilantes.

ALDERMAN FREAKO: Oh, I think that's going too far. We have to be able to defend ourselves *(he draws a large knife out of his sleeve and chuckles)*

Boos and cheers from the floor.

SOCIAL WORKER: Just a minute, # 5 of our G.A.R.P. is that we should respect the right of all burglars to earn a living and feed their families. Families, families, yes, yes, yes, families. Doesn't that clinch the argument. They must support their families. Otherwise, burglars will have to take to crimes . . .

ALDERMAN FATSO: *(interrupting)* But burglary is a crime . . .

SOCIAL WORKER: *(interrupting)* Please let me finish! I was going to say *(she pauses intently)* If burglars cannot feed their families, they will take to crimes much worse than mere stealing -

such as violent robbery, robbery with murder. Crimes of smuggling, slashing, terrorism, extortion, blackmail and so on. Therefore, we must at least give them a fair chance to carry out their relatively harmless burglaries.

Raising her voice above the boos and jeers and the hoorays and cheers.

In fact, G.A.R.P. # 6 says that householders should always leave lying about a decent sum of money in cash - so as to give any stray burglar an incentive to get out of your home real quick - otherwise he might set fire to it or otherwise wreck it in disgust.

TOWNSWOMAN: *(to the nearest burglars on the stage)* Oh, so you'll burn down my house will you? *(lifts up an umbrella or stick and strides over to the burglar's side)* Burn me out if I don't give you protection money will you?

CHAIRMAN BURGLAR: Ma'am that's a misrepresentation of what was said. Nobody wants to burn your house. All you do is leave some money around your house just in case a burglar needs it for his family.

More boos and cheers as the two sides begin to roll up their sleeves and show signs of eventually coming to blows.

Let's have a brief intermission so that we can discuss all this in peace and quiet and come to an honest agreement between us. After all, we're bringing money into the town now by holding this convention here. So there are two sides to every debate. Money is money and money talks and who cares where the money comes from so long as we get it.

He sings: **GOLD BUGS**

Sung: Jerkily and Cheerfully

VERSE 1:

d f l f d f l f
We shovel and slave, we rant and rave
d - d f f f m r m f s
As we scratch each patch for the wealth we crave
d f l f d f l f
Ho, ho, hee, hee, ho, ho, hee, hee
l d^1 l s s f
We'll bug all day for gold
d f l - l f d f l f
It's more than a joke, we've all gone broke
d f f - f - f m - r m - f s
It's not just a fad, we're raving mad
d f l f d f l f
Ho, ho, hee, hee, ho, ho, hee, hee
l d^1 l s s f
We'll bug all day for gold

VERSE 1:
We shovel and slave, we rant and rave
As we scratch each patch for the wealth we crave
Ho, ho, hee, hee, ho, ho, hee, hee
We'll bug all day for gold
It's more than a joke, we've all gone broke
It's not just a fad, we're raving mad
Ho, ho, hee, hee, ho, ho, hee, hee
We'll bug all day for gold.

REFRAIN:
Some little bugs come, some big bugs go
That's just the way of the world you know
But the only bugs who never grow old
Are the bugs who bug for gold
Smash up the stones, give them a kick
One more shovel load might do the trick
Ho, ho, hee, hee, ho, ho, hee, hee
We bug all day for gold.

VERSE 2:
And when we've found the gold we love
We'll bug some more for treasure trove
Ho, ho, hee, hee, ho, ho, hee, hee
We'll bug for treasure trove
The search for treasure never ends
We may strut all around and impress our friends
Ho, ho, hee, hee, ho, ho, hee, hee
Then we'll bug for treasure trove.

VERSE 3:
If you live in hope you'll never grow old
It'll keep you alive just a digging for gold
Ho, ho, hee, hee, ho, ho, hee, hee
We'll bug for silver and gold
But when we've made our very last try
We'll dig some more in the sweet bye and bye
Ho, ho, hee, hee, ho, ho, hee, hee
We're bugs for treasure trove.

As townsfolk continue to protest.

Look, we've heard the Burglars' Union Social Worker. After we all calm down and have a nice break we'll hear what the townsfolk have to say. We'll hear both sides before we set up a policy document. All right. Is that fair?

The two sides calm down somewhat but are still arguing with each other as they mill around, taking a short break.

Curtain

SCENE THREE - WORKINGMAN SOLIDARITY

The same scene as before with the same groups of burglars and townsfolk filing back into their seats but this time they are shaking fists and walking sticks and umbrellas and coshes and jimmies and flashlights at each other.

CHAIRMAN BURGLAR: Calm down now. I promised that the townsfolk would have a chance to make their case. And yes, I'm a man of my word. Mayor Jellybelly, it's your turn now to comment on our proposed policy based on G.A.R.P. You did approve the plan before this meeting, right?

MAYOR: Well, when I heard about Generally Accepted Rehabilitation Principles, I thought that rehabilitation meant putting rogues back into life after prison and putting honest reformed thieves out to hard graft and work like the rest of us - that was my mistake, of course. I know now that modern rehabilitation means keeping them out of prison at all costs. Now that's all right only so long as they go out and earn an honest living.

VOICE OF BURGLAR: But my resume is so bad, how can I get a job? It upsets even me and I wrote it!

MAYOR: If reading over your resume doesn't make you feel great - you're just not a good enough liar and whose fault is that?

ANOTHER VOICE: I cannot tell a lie. I confess freely it wasn't me - it was him over there.

MAYOR: Shut up. Shut up. Shut up.

Cheers from townsfolk.

BURGLAR SECRETARY: But surely you understand Mayor, people will not give us jobs and we still have to feed our families.

MAYOR: Well, there's jobs that don't need honesty - like digging power-line trenches *(howls of anger from the burglars)* or flying airplanes *(subdued growls from burglars)* or TV evangelist, or media moron but the point is sometimes it's a toss up whether we stop you from feeding your families or whether you stop us from feeding ours - by ripping us off. So we just have to find reasonable compromises.

I propose therefore that the Generally Accepted Rehabilitation Principles should be rejected by the meeting as being too one-sided in favor of burglars. Let us have a minute for discussion and then we'll vote on it and whichever side wins the vote - that decision will be officially accepted by the convention meeting. All right.

Everyone nods - mayor smiles kindly.

Good, good. No hard feelings. No crude yelling or shouting or insulting.

Everyone, somewhat reluctantly but sincerely nods in agreement.

No arguments. Just an orderly, democratic, intelligent vote, straight up or down, to accept G.A.R.P. or not O.K?

Everyone brightens and relaxes and agrees.

Make your decision known. Yes or No on these slips of paper. It's either - Make life easy for burglars "YES" to avoid worse crises or "NO" do not, O.K.? *(all smile and agree)* Let's just pass out the voting slips then *(pleased with himself)* I'm a fervent believer in democracy myself - democracy . . .

While the voting slips are being passed out, the bugler reappears, dressed as before, bugle in hand, at front stage.

BUGLER: Democracy, yes, yes, truly so. Buglers of the World at this great Annual Convention. I am a true member of your union. It cannot possibly be burglars - that is clearly a typo, a mere technical printing error, in short, a mistake - in fact rubbish. It is all a great misrepresentation. I am a truly professional bugler and should be admitted. You must hear what I can do with this old bugle, then you will want to admit me in the name of true democracy. Listen to my proof of full eligibility for membership. Listen, I truly represent the working classes at skilled labor level.

Remember this, the International of all the Buglers has a duty to represent every properly apprenticed and journeyman bugler in order to protect his skills from exploitation by big biz, big gubmint or big gunz and in order to prevent his loss of livelihood to untrained and unlicensed scab labor. *Sings:*

DRINK YOUR TEA

Sung: Jolly

VERSE 1:

d d d d l_1 - d
Don't get scared or skittish
f f f r - f
Fight to the finish
d d d d r - d
Be proud to be British
d l_1 s_1
Drink your tea.
d d d d l_1 - d
No matter how you suffer
f f f f r - f
Keep a true stiff upper
f f f f m - m
Eat a good fish supper
f s f
Drink your tea.

VERSE 1:

Don't get scared or skittish
Fight to the finish
Be proud to be British
Drink your tea.
No matter how you suffer
Keep a true stiff upper
Eat a good fish supper
Drink your tea.

VERSE 2:
Don't let worries hook you
Don't let life rebuke you
Let's all go cuckoo
Drinking tea, drinking tea.
Let's not get flappie
Let's not be snappy
Let's all be happy
Drink your tea.

VERSE 3:
Now working lads and lasses
Never fear the asses
Of the upper classes
Drinking tea, drinking tea
Fight them to the finish
Don't get scared or skittish
Remember we're British
Drink your tea, drink your tea.

The class struggle can only be won if all and sundry truly qualified apprenticed labor are permitted to join the union. I have no objection to paying the full union dues commensurate with my earning capacity *(thinks, shrugs)* which is nil anyway. Furthermore, comrades, I am one of those who call to arms the sons and daughters of the proletarian revolution to overthrow, by workingman solidarity, the despicable capitalist despots of the western world. Listen . . . Listen comrades.

His hearers are stunned and confused as the bugler plays a cavalry charge on his horn - this can be a record played from back or side stage - chaos breaks out and both sides attack each other vigorously, using all available weapons.

BUGLER: Stop, listen, do not kill each other on account of poor me. Hear what I can do.

He continues bugling a charge as both sides attack each other and shout GARP for ever or GARP is GARBAGE. A total melee takes place as the bugle call and the fighting continues.

FINALE: *All three songs in Scene One, Two and Three are now sung in their order of appearance.*

Curtain

END OF PLAYSCRIPT

APPENDIX
FIVE FINGER EXERCISE
Simple Instructions on How to Play the Tunes

Music is presented in the form of tonic sol-fa. Tonic sol-fa is the written form of music for both beginners and virtuosos – those who do not need guidance on timing, arrangements or chords – those who need only the basic tune.

1. Hitting the Right Note
2. White Keys - Stick-On Labels
3. Black Keys - Stick-On Labels
4. Getting the Timing Right
5. Summary

HITTING THE RIGHT NOTE

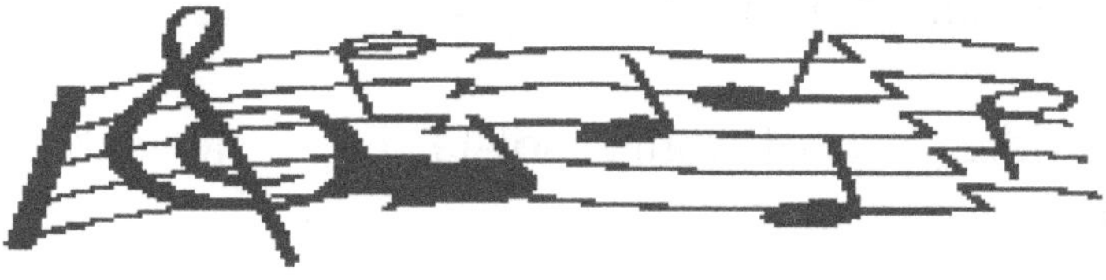

C is the white note just to the left of the two black notes side by side. Find Middle C on your keyboard. A register is the level of a set of tonic sol-fa. Here is the location of Middle C on a standard three register keyboard. The white note in the exact middle of any keyboard is Middle C (in staff) and Doh (in tonic sol-fa).

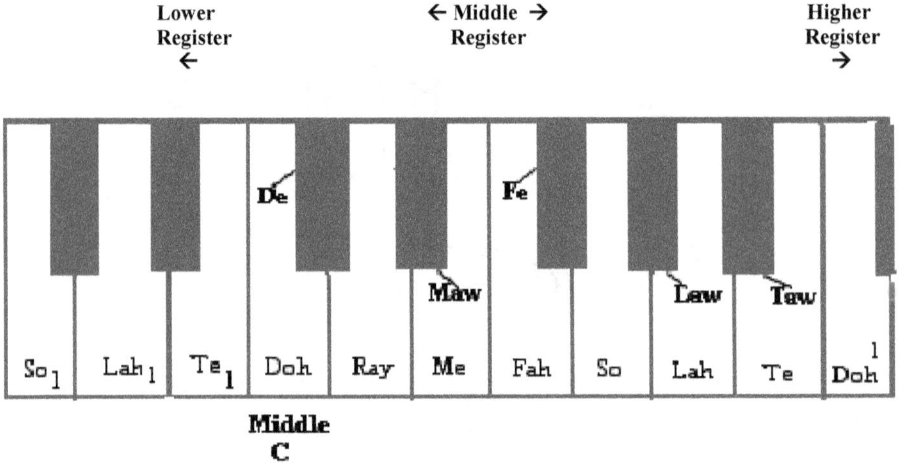

The tunes in this songbook can all be played on these three middle registers. Larger keyboards may have additional higher or lower registers but these will not be needed for the simple basic tunes in this book.

C is always Doh and going up from Middle C is the central set of tonic sol-fa - Doh, Ray, Me, Fah, Soh, Lah, Te.
The next note is also a C and is the Doh higher than Central Doh. This starts off the next register of tonic sol-fa notes.

The Middle Set of tonic sol-fa have no subscript or superscript: d, r, m, f, s, l, t.

The Lower Register (set of tonic sol-fa) have subscripts as follows: d_1, r_1, m_1, f_1, s_1, l_1, t_1.

The Higher Register (set of tonic sol-fa) have superscripts as follows: d^1, r^1, m^1, f^1, s^1, l^1, t^1.

Here is a complete set of labels, for the white and black keys, to stick onto your central basic keyboard.

WHITE KEYS: STICK-ON LABELS FOR YOUR KEYBOARD

LOWER REGISTER	Doh_1	Ray_1	Me_1	Fah_1	Soh_1	Lah_1	Te_1
MIDDLE REGISTER	Doh	Ray	Me	Fah	Soh	Lah	Te
HIGHER REGISTER	Doh^1	Ray^1	Me^1	Fah^1	Soh^1	Lah^1	Te^1

WHITE STICK-ON NOTE INSTRUCTIONS

These are to be stuck on to your keyboard to show you which notes to play as you follow the Tonic Sol-fa music set out in each song.

1. The seven white notes with subscripts (lower register) lead up to Middle C.
2. Middle C starts off the middle register of seven white notes that have neither subscripts nor superscript.
3. The seven white notes with superscripts (higher register) follows on after the middle register.

Only the last three white notes of the lower register and the first white note of the higher register are shown with the middle register in the above diagram *(p. 386)*.

THE BLACK KEYS

The black keys in each register are as follows:

de, maw, fe, law, taw.

The five black keys in the lower register
have subscripts
The five black keys in the middle register
have no subscripts or superscripts
The five black keys in the higher register
have superscripts.

Here are the three sets of labels to stick onto the black notes on your keyboard.

LOWER REGISTER	**De_1**	**Maw_1**	**Fe_1**	**Law_1**	**Taw_1**
MIDDLE REGISTER	**De**	**Maw**	**Fe**	**Law**	**Taw**
HIGHER REGISTER	**De^1**	**Maw^1**	**Fe^1**	**Law^1**	**Taw^1**

GETTING THE TIMING RIGHT

(1) Notes that are grouped together have hyphens between them - to show that they are played together.
(eg: d - f - l). This does not mean that such notes are speeded up, only that they are joined together.
(2) Notes that are to be held longer than average are written in italics - that is to say they are sloped to the right (eg: *d* or *s*).
(3) Try to follow the hints at the head of each tune
(eg: slow and simple or fast and warlike).
(4) Keep a steady and regular beat whether the tune is fast or slow (eg: tap your foot or get a friend to tap out an even measured beat).

SUMMARY

Below is a diagram of all three registers - Lower, Middle and Higher. Of course, on many keyboards and pianos there are more than these three registers but these keys are all that you will need to play the simple tunes in this songbook

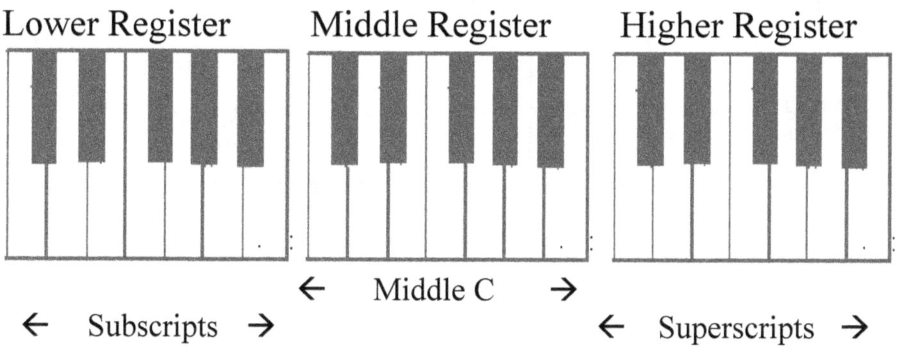

BRIEF INSTRUCTIONS

1. Cut out the squares and stick them on to the black and white keys.
2. Hit the notes asked for in the tonic sol-fa tunes, trying to hear each melody as a whole and keeping a steady beat.

Key to Tonic Sol-fa Notes

D = doh
R = ray
M = me
F = fah
S = soh
L = lah
T = te

WHITE KEYS: STICK-ON LABELS FOR YOUR KEYBOARD

LOWER REGISTER	Doh_1	Ray_1	Me_1	Fah_1	Soh_1	Lah_1	Te_1
MIDDLE REGISTER	Doh	Ray	Me	Fah	Soh	Lah	Te
HIGHER REGISTER	Doh^1	Ray^1	Me^1	Fah^1	Soh^1	Lah^1	Te^1

BLACK KEYS: STICK-ON LABELS FOR YOUR KEYBOARD

LOWER REGISTER	De_1	Maw_1	Fe_1	Law_1	Taw_1
MIDDLE REGISTER	De	Maw	Fe	Law	Taw
HIGHER REGISTER	De^1	Maw^1	Fe^1	Law^1	Taw^1

HOW TO IMPROVE YOUR SINGING

In singing these songs there are seven main aspects of singing to check out and practice towards perfection. (There are also several more subtle, complex and minor aspects which only a real-life music teacher could explain. Each aspect of singing calls for separate exercises as well as putting all six together.

1. Voice Quality

Largely a given, quality can be developed by practice, healthy diet and deep breathing.

2. Diction

Concentrate on sharp clear pronunciation to achieve understanding on the part of the listener. Aim for sounds that most people with standard English, not accents, will understand.

3. Projection

Throw out the voice until all the audience can hear it. Every word must always reach the listener.

4. Phrasing

A phrase is a group of words and notes that are grouped together. Watch how the sounds and words hang together and change the combinations until it sounds right to you in your opinion. What is right for one singer may not be right for another.

5. Feeling

Try to imagine how the sender of the message would feel and think. Develop a dramatic empathy, a oneness with the message of the song so that it comes over as genuine.

6. Rhythm

Keep an even beat or a creative subtly uneven one. Tap your foot on the ground or follow a drummer, or hand claps (see also the section on timing).

7. True Notes

Make sure that the note you play is the right one. Listen to a self-tape and compare your notes with those sung by a friend or played on a keyboard or other instrument. Sometimes it helps to close your eyes and listen well.

8. Find a Teacher

If you can, find a good singing teacher with top credentials or at least get a musical friend to critique you.

THE END

www.ingramcontent.com/pod-product-compliance
Lightning Source LLC
Chambersburg PA
CBHW051812090426
42736CB00011B/1448
* 9 7 8 0 9 5 6 1 4 3 5 3 2 *